Defenders of the Heart

Hay House Titles of Related Interest

Defenders of the Heart

Managing the Habits and
Attitudes That Block You from
a Richer, More Satisfying Life

MARILYN KAGAN, LCSW
and
NEIL EINBUND, Ph.D.

HAY HOUSE, INC.
Carlsbad, California • New York City
London • Sydney • Johannesburg
Vancouver • Hong Kong • New Delhi

Published and distributed in the United States by: Hay House, Inc.: www.
hayhouse.com • *Published and distributed in Australia by:* Hay House
Australia Pty. Ltd.: www.hayhouse.com.au • *Published and distributed
in the United Kingdom by:* Hay House UK, Ltd.: www.hayhouse.co.uk •
Published and distributed in the Republic of South Africa by: Hay House
SA (Pty), Ltd.: www.hayhouse.co.za • *Distributed in Canada by:* Raincoast:
www.raincoast.com • *Published in India by:* Hay House Publishers India:
www.hayhouse.co.in

Design: Tricia Breidenthal

Library of Congress Cataloging-in-Publication Data

Kagan, Marilyn.
  Defenders of the heart : managing the habits and attitudes that block
you from a richer, more satisfying life / Marilyn Kagan and Neil Einbund.
     p. cm.
  ISBN 978-1-4019-2037-1 (tradepaper : alk. paper) 1. Defense
mechanisms (Psychology) 2. Success--Psychological aspects. 3. Self-
actualization (Psychology) 4. Self-help techniques. I. Einbund, Neil,
1960- II. Title.
  BF175.5.D44K34 2008
  158--dc22

                                               2008021489

ISBN: 978-1-4019-2037-1

11 10 09 08   4 3 2 1
1st edition, November 2008

FSC
Mixed Sources
Product group from well-managed
forests and other controlled sources

Cert no. SW-COC-002283
www.fsc.org
© 1996 Forest Stewardship Council

Printed in the United States of America

To Martin and Dorothy Kagan.
I miss you both more than I ever
thought possible. Thanks, Dad, for
sharing a wacky sense of humor
. . . it's my favorite Defender.

– Marilyn

To Eunice Einbund and Marni Levine.
You left us way too soon, but your loving
hearts continue to touch us all forever.

– Neil

CONTENTS

PREFACE

Defenders of the Heart has been a long time in the making. We—Marilyn and Neil—have a combined 40 years of experience in counseling, as well as providing psychotherapy for people on all sorts of life issues, and we have worked together for much of that time. Allow us to introduce each other to you.

Neil on Marilyn

"Marilyn has been in private practice as a thera-pist in Los Angeles for more than 25 years. Those of you who live in the Southern California area are fortunate, because although you might never have met with her one-on-one, you've had the opportunity to benefit from her droll wit and profound wisdom on radio and television. She brought her undisputed bona fides as a licensed psychotherapist (she got a

master's from the San Diego State University School of Social Work and did postgraduate training at various institutions, including the Southern California Psychoanalytic Institute) to KFI—that's the number one talk radio station in the area, where she reigned for eight years, dispensing advice to callers with care, kindness, and a healthy dose of humor. But radio couldn't contain her, and she naturally gravitated toward television and The Marilyn Kagan Show (Emmy nominated, no less). That show led to her being called upon as a guest expert and commentator on all the major networks and local stations, discussing life issues and patterns that begin in childhood and continue throughout adulthood.

"We probably shouldn't be surprised by her on-air success, because she has a background in performing. In her 20s and early 30s, Marilyn pursued an early dream and starred in local theater, which led to a starring role in the movie Foxes opposite Jodie Foster. She continued to act in films and guest-starred in a number of popular television series, including playing a therapist on Ellen.

"Apart from her professional credentials and media visibility, Marilyn is also a valued member of the community. She was supervising family therapist for eight years at the Linden Center, a residential treatment program for emotionally and physically abused children in L.A. She also co-founded the California Artists Human Services, a nonprofit mental-health organization serving those struggling in the entertainment industry.

"I met Marilyn more than 20 years ago at the University of Judaism (now called American Jewish

University) in L.A., where she was, and still is, work-ing as an instructor for the Making Marriage Work program. We became colleagues and lifelong friends, and are now co-authors. She's the proud mom of a beautiful, sensitive, funny, creative 11-year-old daughter . . . just ask her!"

Marilyn on Neil

"Okay, let's get the big guns out of the way first. Neil is a licensed clinical psychologist and marriage and family therapist. He got his doctorate from the University of Southern California in 1988 and spent several years as a professor for the Master of Arts in Psychology program at Antioch University in Marina del Rey, California. His expertise covers a wide range of specialties, including family dynamics/relation-ships, marriage counseling, addictions, divorce, and grief work.

"Neil has spent the last 20 years teaching in the Making Marriage Work program at the University of Judaism, where we met. He helped shape the curricu-lum for couples who are about to be married. One of his most important activities for the community is his involvement in running weekend grief groups at local cemeteries for people who have recently lost loved ones.

"Although Neil has a wicked sense of humor, he can be a shy and introspective guy sometimes. His wife, Judy, and I think he's adorable; we say he could be a movie star. But the idea of being in front of the camera leaves him in a cold sweat: when his three

energetic and genius kids pull out their video cam-
eras, he heads for the hills. He's the happy dad of a
17-year-old son and 14- and 8-year-old daughters."

Now Back to Our Regularly Scheduled Preface

We've wanted to write a book together for a long
time. Ultimately, we were inspired to pen this one,
Defenders of the Heart, because throughout our years of
treating patients, we have continually come face-to-face
with one universal psychological truth: when we grow
more conscious of our defense mechanisms and begin to
understand how these devices help and hurt us throughout our lives, our world becomes richer and less barren.
We believe that we all should have the opportunity to
delve deeply inside ourselves and become acquainted
with our defenses—even without therapy—for a chance
to live the most rewarding life. So we've chosen what
we've observed to be the ten most common emotional
defense mechanisms, which, we contend, we adopt at a
very young age to deal with a wide variety of new situations and challenges. All of us, at some time or another,
call upon these methods to protect our hearts. We've
coined them *Defenders of the Heart,* and we've developed
strategies for managing them.

In one way or another, overly constructed Defenders of the Heart are at the base of nearly all of our bouts
with dissatisfaction. The hunger for a fuller, more joyful
existence speaks as much to those of us with good families, friends, and health as it does to others facing serious
life challenges. You'll recognize these Defenders in your
partners, family members, friends, and co-workers, just
as you do in yourself.

Over the years, we've worked with thousands of people—ranging from celebrities and top executives of major broadcasting networks to individuals from all walks of life, including students, homemakers, retirees, and young urban professionals. Regardless of their circumstances or history, we find that many have blind spots in their emotional "vision," just as we all do.

Like them, you may have some awareness of the concept of a defense mechanism, but you probably don't realize which ones are affecting your own life or how to escape their self-defeating grip. You want to change your life, yet you can't see the very obvious paths that open before you—paths that can lead to greater clarity.

We wrote *Defenders of the Heart* to give you a strong basic understanding of the most common defense mechanisms, to teach you how to recognize which ones are sabotaging your life, and to provide you with a comprehensive tool set to break free of their life-limiting powers. Think of it as a troubleshooters' guide to our emotional hearts and social selves, designed for us to understand and get a grip on our most common Defenders of the Heart.

The book is organized with a chapter devoted to each of these ten common Defenders of the Heart. The psychological profession has names for them *(Denial, Projection, Rationalization, Intellectualization, Humor, Displacement, Sublimation, Procrastination, Altruism, Passive-Aggression)*, but we'll demystify the jargon to the point where you'll recognize them all too well in yourself and in others.

You'll also be able to walk through exercises, quizzes, tests, interpersonal activities, and straightforward tips to help lower your personal walls. These psychological tools are the result of our decades of work as therapists and reflect tried-and-true methods for helping our patients (and now, you) overcome emotional Defenders of the Heart. These resources have changed many people's lives and will be highly effective for you, too.

In each chapter you'll find a section entitled "Heart Beat." This is where we've included studies, news items, and research that help reinforce our premise. Just as journalists have a "beat"—an area of expertise that they cover—we consider the *heart* our beat as we pass on this information to you.

Important parts of each chapter are the examples of the struggles and victories of a variety of people who illustrate the issues we're discussing. Basically, we take you through the process we usually follow when patients come to us for therapy. That includes learning about their childhoods and their family dynamics, as well as finding out what's going on with them in the present. We'll also identify which events or interactions might have activated Defenders they learned when young, causing them to surface now. In addition, we'll share the exercises and advice we gave them. Naturally, your particular circumstances will be different, but we think reading others' stories will help you understand where your own Defenders might have come from.

The personal accounts you'll read are all true. Due to the nature of our work, we must, of course, preserve the privacy of those involved, so all names have been changed. In a few instances we've even fused some personalities together to better illustrate a point. Almost all of the examples presented here are drawn from the case histories of those we've treated as individuals and in groups. Some whose lives we reveal haven't seen us in therapy, but we've had the good fortune to know them as friends or colleagues.

In addition, we've included the stories of celebrities and others in show business who blazed their own trails while learning how to see and govern their own Defenders of the Heart. They narrate these accounts in their own words, and we call them "Talk Stories," after the Hawaiian tradition of oral storytelling. We devote an entire chapter to these Talk Stories at the end, following our explanation of the ten Defenders. By reading about others' journeys as they became more attentive to how they were living their daily lives, you'll be privy to their development. You'll learn how they reached into themselves to make peace with their Defenders—and, in some cases, actually transformed these habits and attitudes into a resource that worked *for* them rather than against them.

Everyone who appears within the pages of this book has added richness to our lives and to this endeavor. We've entrusted you with our professional and personal stories so that you'll be able to identify situations and feelings that resonate in your own life.

No one would deny that your heart deserves the best protection possible, but you can't lock it away for safekeeping. To thrive—to get enjoyment from living—you must keep your heart in touch with the world: giving and receiving love and reaching out to embrace the people, activities, and causes that create a full life. This is one of the most fundamental tasks for enhancing your psychological well-being. We trust you'll undertake it with a willing heart . . . which will lead you to an *open* heart, and consequently, a bigger experience of life and love. In the end, this is a book about wisdom for the heart— knowing when, where, why, and how to open yours to the many possibilities that invite you into a more complete and deeply satisfying existence.

INTRODUCTION

Think for a moment about your heart. In our culture, we regard it as the place where our feelings and emotions live, and all of us are very concerned about its vulnerability! For decades, popular songs have brimmed with our universally felt fears: from plaintive questions such as "What Becomes of the Brokenhearted?" to poignant pleas like "Un-break My Heart." Who at some time or another hasn't felt they had a "Hungry Heart," been in search of a "Heart of Gold," or been at the mercy of someone else's "Cold, Cold Heart"?

Now if you're like most of us, you think of yourself as a fairly openhearted person. You're kind. You do things for others. You like to think of yourself as trustworthy and giving.

But the truth is that the majority of us are not really as openhearted as we think we are. And there's a good reason for that. Our hearts are precious to us. They deserve to be handled with care and to be protected. So to that end, in our earliest years, we begin arming our emotional hearts with a barrage of protection strategies. This is a necessary step in everyone's development. We equip ourselves with the habits and attitudes without which our hearts would be *too* open, too easily damaged by people and situations that either aren't kind enough or simply aren't right for us and the lives we want to lead. These habits and attitudes are what we call *Defenders of the Heart.*

It's completely natural and necessary to use these Defenders when we're very small children figuring out how to make our way in the world of family, school, and friends. And while they may protect us while we're young, they can actually hurt us in adult life. Unless we become aware of and attentive to them, these Defenders tend to keep on going like a computer program that runs constantly in the background, unseen and limiting our progress. Over time, they become so habitual that they turn into blockades.

On the face of it, these Defenders may appear very different; in fact, they have a commonality of purpose. We're sure you've heard of some of them—*Denial, Humor, Procrastination,* and *Passive-Aggression,* for example—as they've become part of our lexicon (even though sometimes we use them inaccurately). But some that may not be so well known to you are *Projection, Sublimation, Altruism, Displacement, Rationalization,* and *Intellectualization.*

Your Defenders were built at such an early stage of your life that in your adulthood they now feel like second nature. They started growing around your heart to shield you from fears, anxieties, and tensions that you just couldn't bear to feel.

Take the case of Ricky. He was an adorable baby boy. Although Mom and Dad worshipped the ground he crawled on, they had their hands full taking care of him and his two older brothers. When Ricky went down for his nap, Mom focused on her new home business, and Dad hung out with the other children. Around the time Ricky turned one, Mom and Dad began to let him cry a little longer when he woke up than he'd been used to. With this new wrinkle in his life, along with other things both positive and negative happening in his world, Ricky learned a way to defend his heart from disappointment. In order to withstand the discomfort that resulted from Mom and Dad not soothing him when he cried, he turned to his "blankie" more and more. Ricky figured out a way to console himself when he felt the pain of not being immediately gratified.

Like all of us, Ricky found a way to deal with life's disappointments and frustrations. It's a normal thing. As he grew up, these early methods of relating to the world became a part of his personality. Often, without realizing it, he called upon his Defenders of the Heart in times of discomfort and stress.

Now that Ricky has grown into a man, most of the time he can roll with the punches. He's patient, and as a stockbroker, he can easily handle the stress of Wall Street. All his colleagues come to him for support and direction, and his marriage is solid. However, Ricky struggles at times to let his wife know when he feels scared, frustrated, or unsure. When he experiences these feelings, his early-embedded Defender of the Heart comes to the rescue. He turns to himself for solace, like an infant drawing his "blankie" up close, rather than believing he could share some of his vulnerable feelings with his wife and allowing her to comfort him.

Recently, the stock market plummeted, and Ricky felt the sole burden of responsibility. He felt totally alone with his worries and distant from his wife. He was unable to see a precious emotional resource right in front of his eyes—his loving partner, who wanted to be there for him and lighten his load. Ricky was sure that his wife found his current situation too draining and that his feelings would inconvenience her. He was certain she would feel saddled by his difficulties. By allowing his Defender of the Heart to go unchallenged, Ricky lost out on a moment with his wife, who was not only available to soothe him, but deeply wished to be there for her husband. If he could have let her in and stopped projecting his own feelings of shame and neediness onto her, he would have felt a deeper bond with her and less alone. By nurturing this connection with her, his life would have been more complete and meaningful.

Just as with Ricky, your own very clever Defenders continue to be important to you today as your life takes unexpected twists and turns. You must have them to survive, but too much of a good thing becomes a bad one. As a result, you're often unconsciously held in check by Defenders that are working too hard, too often. These overbuilt defenses barricade your heart from trying out newer, better pathways to a rewarding life. They keep you stuck in unsatisfying patterns.

Unfortunately, unless you gain an awareness of them, these defensive habits that you developed long ago can eventually become destroyers of your happiness. Our experience as therapists has shown us that every person we've ever counseled has needed to get a better handle on one or more Defenders of the Heart. The crucial thing to know about them is that over time they become so set in stone that whenever you're faced with upsetting situations, you just keep falling back on them. They seem like normal reactions. However, your entrenched Defenders drain much of the joy from your life and actually can prevent and even destroy all the good feelings they were originally meant to ensure.

There is wonderful news, though. When we've had the privilege of assisting people in learning to recognize their Defenders, they have been able to bring them down to healthy levels. The result is always a fuller heart—a greater sense of peace, achievement, contentment, and fulfillment.

The Caged Heart

All this time, of course, we've been talking about your emotional heart. To help give you a very clear idea of how your Defenders of the Heart often work against you, we want to offer you an illustration that you can wrap your head around. Think for a moment about your actual physical heart: that little red muscular pump in your chest that keeps you alive. How is *it* protected?

Nature has given your physical heart an ingenious shield—a cage of strong yet flexible and lightweight bones. In a term that structural engineers use, your rib cage is "elegant." It does its job with a highly efficient design and just the right amount of materials. But what if your elegant rib cage were overbuilt? Imagine the consequences if it were solid bone.

There actually is a rare and dramatic disease called *Fibrodysplasia ossificans progressiva* that causes bone to form in the wrong places. Over time, it can restrict victims' mobility so much that they resemble stone statues. Unless you're closely related to someone who has this condition, there's very little chance that it would ever attack you. But just consider this for a moment: what would it be like if some strange disease were to put solid bone into all the spaces between your ribs?

First, your body would become heavier to carry around. Second, it would become so rigid that the simple act of bending would be impossible for you. Anytime you wanted to reach for something, you would have to lean with your whole upper body. Lacking normal flexibility, you would also find it much harder to keep your balance.

That is very much like what happens to our emotional selves—usually without our actually realizing it—when our Defenders of the Heart are overbuilt. We carry around stiff armor. We become inflexible. We find it harder to reach for the things we desire. We become socially and emotionally awkward. We must struggle to stay in balance. Most damaging of all, we can't let the very people and experiences we want, need, and love come into our hearts. That's a very limiting way to live, and also very unhealthy. The two of us consider the rigidity of these Defenders of the Heart to be the number one cause of unhappiness, isolation, and disconnection.

Once using our Defenders becomes a lifelong knee-jerk reaction, they work against us. They prevent us from new and fresh experiences, expanding our horizons, making better love relationships, and living a richer existence.

**It's only when you're able to feel the
weight of all of your emotions that you'll
be able to find fulfillment in your life.**

Understand that you're not the only person who feels that a more complete and pleasurable life is somewhere just beyond reach. Dissatisfaction and heartache are really epidemic. Ten million Americans are on antidepressants, and at least one in five suffers from mental illness at some time in life. Costs of illegal-drug abuse are estimated at more than $100 billion annually, with alcohol abuse costing close to twice that much. Nearly always, the people who abuse drugs are "self-medicating" for undiagnosed depression.

We're aware of the various problems and the discontent in our own lives, yet all of us know some people who seem to have it all together. They've got great kids and a mate they're glad to see when the day winds down. Even the dog is happy to see them! They have a job that allows them to pay their monthly bills without cramping their lifestyle. They've been able to enjoy those family trips every year. Perhaps they're even among those lucky or smart ones who have been socking it away for old age or for the kids' college funds. It seems they're where they want to be. They have the good life.

Sure, they may endure the stresses and strains of juggling a busy calendar. They might dream of having more money, a bigger house, a swankier vacation, lower cholesterol, or fewer battles with the kids and spouse at home. They've got just a few bumps in a rather smooth road, but essentially no major potholes. Yet many of these people who live in what appear to be great circumstances have an emptiness in the pits of their stomachs—as if something is still missing in their lives. Questions float in their heads:

- "What's my problem?"

- "Why do I get this despondent, empty feeling?"

- "What's wrong when nothing seems to be wrong?"

- "What could possibly be missing when life looks pretty sweet?"

- "Where is this lack of contentment coming from?"

This yearning to quiet the aching heart is nothing new. Great scholars, deep thinkers, spiritual teachers, and religious leaders through the centuries have all had explanations for this malaise. Despite outward appearances, the fact is, we all have Defenders; and at one time or another they have a hand in giving rise to these kind of questions.

What we've found is that most of us become more enmeshed with one Defender than another, just as our friend Ricky favored Projection (which you'll read about in Chapter 2). Depending on how you react to things that happen in your life as you grow, you may go beyond your most-used Defender and call upon various others to protect you. For example, you might have harnessed Humor (Chapter 5) in high school when you found out that cracking a clever gibe at someone else's expense took away from your feelings of insecurity. Or maybe in order to avoid the pain associated with the crushing defeat of losing your first job in young adulthood, you made an excuse to account for the firing—you pulled out Rationalization (Chapter 3)—rather than feel the terrible blows of rejection.

Knowing more about what your Defenders are and how you use them in certain stressful, anxiety-provoking situations will assist you in becoming the captain of your own destiny. Rather than being ruled by them without any conscious awareness on your part, you'll lower your Defenders and have them serve you instead of block you.

When the Time Is Right

Take, for example, Brian and Jerry, two guys in their late 40s. They don't know one another, but they have a lot in common. Brian is considerably overweight. High blood pressure and heart disease run in his family. Jerry is also obese and is a workaholic. His father has serious type 2 diabetes. Both Brian and Jerry go in for checkups and are told that considering their weight, lifestyles, and family histories, they are disasters waiting to happen.

What does each do about it?

Brian lumbers out of his doctor's office and heads straight to his favorite fast-food hangout. He devours a quick snack—large fries and a shake—and then heads back to work.

Jerry leaves his appointment shaken up. He sits for a while in his car and worries about what his wife and kids would do without him. As he drives back to his office, he seriously begins to consider what changes he must make in order to extend his life.

Two guys. Similar circumstances. Very different reactions.

Brian pushes the prospect of death under the rug. He doesn't allow himself to be impacted by this medical reality, even for a minute. He uses Denial (Chapter 1) of the problem and deals with his stress and fear like he always has: by eating poorly . . . a sure way to shorten his life. His Defender of the Heart is working overtime.

Jerry, on the other hand, allows himself to be impacted by the news from his doctor. Somehow he withstands the anxiety and terror of this diagnosis long enough not to react by pushing the news away. He commits to taking action to avert disaster. His Defender of the Heart, also Denial, has weakened. And that's a good thing.

So why did Jerry leave his physical exam dealing with the results in such a different way than Brian did? Because he was *willing* to be affected. He was *willing* and gutsy enough to allow himself to be stirred up. He was *willing* to endure his feelings of discomfort and fear, to really feel them. He let his guard down because he was, as the old saying goes, just sick and tired of being sick and tired. Jerry was ready to have an open heart. This uncovered, unencumbered part of him was poised to expose what is most meaningful to him. He was prepared to react differently than he might have reacted before.

Most of us act more like Brian. Much of the time we walk away from a troubling event unchanged, unaffected. We're *unwilling* to let ourselves be affected. Whether we know it or not, we spend a big chunk of our lives fending off scary, uncomfortable, unfamiliar feelings. But if we try, we can act more like Jerry. We can learn from our own particular life circumstances what's most important to us. We can notice what we feel and then begin to *heal.*

We all have our own pace, our own timetable according to which we're ready to make changes. Some of us get kicked in the gut by a traumatic event and are ready to turn over a new leaf. Others have small negative experiences that just build up on top of one another until we can't take the weight of them anymore and are ready to slough them off. Then there are those who simply wait until Monday or the start of the new year to make changes.

There is no right or wrong time, just *your* time. When you're ready, you'll grab for the brass ring of life. And since you've committed to reading this book, we're fairly certain that you're likely to be in a head space similar to Jerry's—ready to take that leap from inaction to action and finally enjoy a life filled with satisfaction and joy.

As we develop an ability to tolerate our own feelings and look at them without being afraid, we eventually realize something very powerful: we have a choice of how we want to fill the void in our lives . . . or, as in the case of Jerry, to avoid disaster.

Of course, it's not easy to make this transformation—to "downsize" your Defender of the Heart. Half a millennium ago, Shakespeare wrote: "Men's faults do seldom to themselves appear." And those words are just as true today: Defenders of the Heart are rarely revealed without the aid of another. Think of this book as your "another."

With the stories and exercises in these pages, you'll begin moving toward freedom. By sampling the experiences of others, you'll see glimpses of yourself and of the ways you might start to find greater satisfaction in your life. You'll gain access to your heart. With that, you'll be kinder to, and more forgiving of, yourself; and, in turn, a generosity of spirit toward others will have room to flourish. The upshot of all of this is that your life will truly be more vibrant. And then, to end as we began— with a song—you'll be living "Heart and Soul."

Chapter One

Face Your Fear and Doubt: Dial Down *Denial*

Defendapedia

De·ni·al (*di-NAHY-uhl*): The tactic of overlooking the obvious to reduce anxiety.

Denial heads up our list of Defenders of the Heart. And no wonder. It's the premier, *el numero uno,* the big kahuna, the Kilimanjaro of the entire ten—all for good reason. The most commonly used Defender of the Heart, Denial influences every area of life. The other Defenders also have elements of pushing aside, dismissing, postponing, and/or ignoring your feelings: there's a kernel of Denial at the core of all of them. Although each Defender is unique, every last one uses a little Denial in the service of allowing you to believe that you can make it through the day.

And let's have a reality check here. Not everything in this world can be hunky-dory every day for any of us. Oh, you know that already? We do, too. Yes, life is filled with pain, suffering, bad times, frustrating challenges, and just plain awful moments. *Ouch!* Not an upbeat way to start out thinking about happiness and that key to greater satisfaction you're about to uncover. Ironically, though, only when you come face-to-face with life's harsh, grim realities can you squeeze out that amazing, wonderful, special, glorious, monumental, awe-inspiring, fulfilled existence you're striving for.

But you grow scared when you imagine getting hurt or disappointed, or when things aren't going well and you're not sure of the outcome. Rather than dealing with the overwhelming, painful circumstances and uncomfortable feelings head-on, you reject them and act as though they never happen. You think that if you meet these bogeymen—these unknown, hidden monsters—face-to-face, the consequence of doing so will be that somewhere inside yourself, you'll crumble and disintegrate into a pile of ashes.

Bogeymen show up in so many different ways. For you it could mean a visit to the doctor with that persistent skin condition you've been ignoring for months, getting on the scale after your pants size has been increasing every month for the last year, finally heeding your girlfriend's roller-coaster outbursts, or facing the reality that your son is coming home late on school days and seems agitated and distant. Whether real or imaginary, your particular bogeyman induces fear in you. Who wants to go eye-to-eye with their bogeyman? Just knowing that it's out there is sometimes plain terrifying. Perhaps you worry that you won't know how to cope with the problem or situation and the feelings it engenders.

So what do you do to make certain you'll dodge these disappointments, heartaches, and fears? What do you do to assure yourself that you're not going to let anything stand in the way of your feeling great? You put up a very clever, seductive roadblock that may, for the moment—and that's the operative phrase, *for the moment*—protect your heart from letdowns, frustrations, worries, and pain. By doing so, you set your feelings aside and use that true-blue Defender of the Heart: Denial.

While Denial does you a major disservice by ignoring and dismissing, sometimes it serves a great function: to protect and defend. In fact, without your fine friend Denial, you would be like an open wound, just asking for an infection!

When Denial Does Good

Denial allows you to keep going when threatened with complete obliteration. It gives you permission to survive in the face of insurmountable odds. Think about the loving couple who has been together 30 years. When the husband drops dead without warning, the wife must plan his entire funeral without skipping a beat. Only by cloaking herself in some Denial is she able to survive the initial heartache. A few weeks after the funeral, she is alone in a quiet space and her deep grief breaks through. Denial had been her comrade that marched with her through "things that had to get done." Now it takes a backseat to the feelings she has to experience.

It's not just during major life events that Denial can serve us. We use it in the day-to-day world as well. For instance, to get to our therapy office, we drive the busiest freeways in the world. Los Angeles is a city where cars are whizzing by at an alarming 80 miles per hour. If we weren't in some state of Denial every day, there's no way we could even make it out the door and into traffic.

Just about everyone is aware of the risks associated with driving: you could get a flat tire; a rock could break your windshield; you could get a speeding ticket; or God forbid, you could have a serious accident. But you can't live minute by minute in that acute state of awareness. So Denial comes in handy by allowing you to get behind the wheel. You would feel way too vulnerable if every moment you were thinking, *What if . . . ?!* You're able to drive because you've actively made a decision to put aside the realities for a time and take the leap. It becomes second nature, and you don't even think, *Oh, now I'm going to shut out the dangers of driving.* But here you are, using this Defender of the Heart in a healthy way.

Denial is not sitting at the forefront of your mind. It's like breathing: you know (or in the case of Denial, you *think*) you must do it to survive, but you really don't pay much attention to it until it's compromised. This Defender of the Heart can be a lifesaver, getting you through the uncomfortable aspects of your life when necessary.

However, as with all Defenders, so often this one becomes a major impediment to greater life satisfaction when it consistently inhibits you from being connected to your feelings. Used for that purpose, Denial is dangerous because it keeps you isolated from those around you and, even more important, from your own wants, needs, and desires, impacting your ability to flourish. That's the unhealthy use of this Defender.

All Evidence to the Contrary

When any Defender of the Heart is doing its job, it's going to turn you away from feelings you're petrified to experience. If it's effective, you won't sense the discomfort. Unhealthy Denial, like the healthy kind, is in the business of squelching feelings. However, this type of Denial is a flight into complete refusal to see your behavior or the consequences at hand. It's living in self-delusion.

Take the guy who says, "I only drink once in a while and can stop anytime I choose." He refuses to see that he grabs for a cocktail immediately upon walking through his front door after work. He's a guy who's disconnected from his own feelings and often from those of others around him.

Our patient Tom was just such a guy—someone who used a form of unhealthy Denial to skirt the underlying fears he'd been living with. Tom was 44 years old and had withstood a tough childhood. Although he'd known that his parents would have laid down their lives for him and his sister, his dad had always been an anxious, unhappy man who frequented the pubs of Boston almost every night. According to Tom, his mother was a "saint." She knew her husband was a hard drinker, but she always made excuses for him. She took up the slack when he would disappoint the kids and did double duty at Tom's wrestling matches and his sister's school plays. When not drinking, Tom's dad was cold, and restricted with his emotions. However, on occasion he was able to let his son in on how guilty he felt about his absences. Tom had vowed that when he had a family, he would never drink to excess.

Tom was a quiet guy like his dad, but with a wicked sense of self-deprecating humor. His sweetness and clever slant on life were what bound Rachel, his wife of 14 years, to him. Over the last few years, his parents had both passed away. His sister lived 3,000 miles away in their hometown, leaving Tom missing her and feeling sadness that his 12-year-old daughter, Jessie, had little contact with his side of the family. Because of a great job opportunity ten years previously, Tom had moved to Los Angeles. He envisioned a happy and prosperous life for himself and his family. But recently his professional life had started going downhill.

The tougher his work was going, the more evenings were spent with "just one more Scotch to take the edge off a crappy day." And then the evening drinking was further supplemented by lunchtime martinis. Yet when you spoke to him, Tom constantly minimized his alcohol consumption.

Tom's employer had recently started outsourcing a lot of the computer troubleshooting for Fortune 500 companies that Tom used to do in-house. Tom was scared that before too long he would go the way of the dinosaur. But he was split off from his worries about his job. He was stuck in a place where he felt that it was "unmanly" to complain (shades of his father) or share his anxieties with anyone, especially Rachel and Jessie.

Tom was drinking more than he ever had, and his family was frightened by his changing personality and growing disconnection from them. Tom had a classic case of Denial. He was refusing to acknowledge what was happening or what *would* happen if he continued along this path.

Like many people who live with loved ones who are using alcohol or drugs to anesthetize their pain and suffering, Rachel got to a place where she couldn't tolerate her husband's behavior. She, too, came from an alcoholic household: her mother would be sleeping on the couch when Rachel came home from school, so she knew first-hand how damaging an addiction could be to a family. She'd been paying close attention to the increase in Tom's drinking and eventually got to her breaking point. She gave him an ultimatum: if he didn't seek help and change his ways, she and Jessie would leave.

Listen to those around you. Whenever loved ones, colleagues, or acquaintances tell you more than twice of their concern about your attitudes, ways of living, or behaviors, you can be sure there's a real problem. We call this *candor contact*. If you don't address these issues, the problem will usually grow. But when you do tackle them, chances are that *you* will grow, which is obviously the much better outcome.

So, still into his full-blown Denial, Tom came in for therapy and, although reticent at first, began working with us. After establishing a safe relationship with him, we were struck by how entrenched he was in his Defender. He didn't think his drinking was any big deal. Furthermore, he had no concept that his work fears had anything to do with his boozing. We knew we had a big job ahead of us. Getting him to admit his worries would be a first step in breaking through his strongly rooted Defender. Somehow we needed to figuratively get inside his heart and awaken it to the fears that were cutting him off from living a fuller life.

**In order to break down Denial, it's
imperative that you begin to be conscious
of what's really unsettling you.**

In our first few meetings, we noticed how broken
and sad Tom seemed. When we pointed this out to him,
he was both surprised and relieved that someone actually noticed the depth of his despair. Tom felt we understood, and this contact allowed us to nonjudgmentally
ask questions concerning both his past and present. We
empathized with him over the way things change so rapidly in our world today. We explored what these changes
meant for him and had him brainstorm other possible
ideas if his work went south.

While talking with him about his own childhood
with an alcoholic father, we made a link for him. How
hard it must have been to be a kid who loved a dad who
appeared to be more interested in the bottle than him.
Finding this pain inside himself, Tom began to wonder
how Jessie must feel about *her* father coming home and
drinking every night. We were able to provide Tom with
a safe place where he could begin to be aware that he
even *had* feelings that were distressing him.

With this secure spot to work in, Tom was able to
open up to what was bothering him the most. To help
facilitate this faster, he needed to pay attention to his
gut, to his physical sensations: the tightness in his chest,
the shallow breathing, and the sore throat that had been
plaguing him for months.

Tom finally got on the same page with us. Within a
safe and supportive environment, he was experiencing
revelations and tolerance both with us and within himself. Tom's clever insights, coupled with his wittiness,

were flourishing once again. Playfully, he conceded that he actually had some feelings he wasn't honoring. After all, he was the one who joked about being "choked up," and maybe that was the cause of his sore throat! So we grabbed him by his fancy lapels and helped him enter the next stage:

We needed Tom to ask himself the hard questions. He had to inquire—of himself and of those around him—what the heck was going on. Along with his loved ones, he had to make a detailed account of:

1. When his drinking began

2. The frequency of the behavior: how often, when, and where he drank

3. The progression of the act—how the drinking had increased over the last year

4. The consequences of his behavior (in this case, his drinking) on his health, finances, friendships, job, marriage, and child

By now, are you starting to get an uncomfortable feeling that *you* have something in common with Tom? What is your "drug" of choice? Do you also anesthetize yourself with alcohol? Or in your case is it food? Pills? Gambling? Sex? Internet porn? Shopping? If so, you need to answer the questions we asked Tom.

It was important that Tom not just do an internal investigation, because—remember—he was in Denial and might be less than honest. An external investigation—experiencing a "candor contact" with those who meant the most to him—was even more critical. For Tom this was a crucial moment in getting a handle on his Defender of the Heart. By questioning his loved ones and being in sync with his bodily feelings, he was able to be affected by Rachel's and Jessie's answers in a way he had never been before. No longer could he deny that his behavior had a profound effect on those he loved.

This was the real start of Tom's progress working on his major Defender of the Heart. His Denial was getting flimsier. His awareness of himself and his behaviors was coming to the forefront of his mind. And for the first time, he was able to talk to Rachel, and us, about how the uncertainty of his work situation frightened him. He began connecting his underlying fears to his excessive drinking. Not only did he stop feeling that it was "unmanly" to share this with Rachel, but just the opposite: he began to feel stronger and surer of himself inside.

In all our years of practice, one certainty has been reinforced for us over and over again: when you share your humiliating and shameful feelings, their power diminishes and you become stronger and more capable.

With Tom's newfound strength, we told him it was imperative that he now pay attention to his daily schedule. Coming home in the evening had been the biggest trigger for him over the past year. Uncorking a bottle was his way to isolate and turn toward himself. Work lunches also triggered his anxiety and worries, so martinis became his soothing friends. He needed to notice how he felt at these times and what was happening both to his body and inside his head. He had to acknowledge those uncomfortable thoughts and feelings that urged him to retreat to old behaviors.

Tom had to find new ways to tolerate and cope with these prickly feelings. It was critical that he experience new avenues in which to "deal." Instead of isolating himself with drink, he committed himself to spending some time with Rachel every night when he walked through the door. Tom began to attend Alcoholics Anonymous meetings during the week. He also returned to activities that used to make him feel alive and connected, such as rejoining a men's softball league that he had been a part of years before.

Tom was willing to experience his life in ways that reinforced that he was a valuable human being despite work issues that were beyond his control. Facing his personal bogeyman, breaking through his fears, and bringing them out into the open wasn't as intimidating as he imagined. And the greatest part of stepping out of his Denial was his ability to take his life back and envision other possibilities.

Tom stayed with his company for another year. He realized that he would never be comfortable in such an unstable environment, so he began an unhurried exploration of other job opportunities that might suit him better. Although looking for new work was stressful, he was able to pay attention to what he had learned about himself, his body's clues, and what was most important to him—namely, his ability to be a dependable husband and father. No longer could Tom ignore the fact that alcohol had had a deep impact not only on his past but also his present.

With Tom, we used the following template that you can work with at home. Although it takes time and effort (and anything worth its salt does), it's a very powerful resource you can use as a springboard toward understanding your own Denial.

Feel, Inquire, Notice, and Experience

The refrain of the unconscious tactic of Denial is: "I'm fine, we're fine, everything's fine." If you notice yourself "singing" those words more times than you or others might like, here's a **F-I-N-E** exercise:

<u>F</u>eel

Check out your body: it's the holding tank of your stress, tension, joy, and sadness. Once you start paying attention to your physical self, you can actually tune in to feelings buried deep within. Say yes or no to the following:

- I frequently get tension headaches.

- I grind my teeth and clench my jaw, sometimes even in my sleep.

- I tend to have a stiff neck and sore shoulders.

- My throat often feels tight, and my voice is raspy.

- I have clammy hands or generally sweat a lot.

- I suffer from gastrointestinal symptoms such as indigestion, heartburn, or diarrhea.

- It doesn't take much to get my heart racing.

- My breathing is often shallow and rapid.

- I have trouble falling and staying asleep.

- I'm often too fatigued for activities I used to enjoy.

- I've lost my libido.

If you answered yes to four or more of these statements and your doctor has ruled out any possible underlying medical conditions, your body may be giving you a clear message that there's something going on in your life that you're not paying attention to.

Try doing this progressive relaxation technique to tune in to—and relieve stress in—some of the areas where you might be holding tension:

1. Find a quiet place where you won't be interrupted for about 15 minutes. Turn off the phone. Get into a comfortable sitting or lying position. You might want to put a light blanket or throw over you.

2. Close your eyes and take some long, slow, deep breaths. Counting to five on each inhalation and each exhalation may help you stay focused.

3. Now start bringing your awareness to your feet. Do you feel any sensations of tightness, tingling, or soreness? Do they ache? Are they tender or hot? As you breathe out, consciously relax the muscles in this area. If you like, wiggle your toes and tense your feet for a moment; then let the tension go as you exhale.

4. Move on up your body in this fashion—from your ankles, calves, thighs, hips, belly, chest, back, shoulders, fingers and arms, and neck . . . all the way to your face and scalp. When you get to any area that's tight or painful, linger there, breathing out the tension before you move on. Be particularly attentive to the small muscles around your jaw, mouth, and eyes, as they're areas that are prone to tightness. Once you become more conscious, you'll realize just how much you're clenching your teeth and "scrunching up" your eyes. As you relax each part of your body, just let it succumb to gravity.

5. Once you've made it all the way through your body, gradually start to stir, and come back into an awareness of your surroundings. Try to carry that feeling of relaxation and openness with you throughout the day.

If you find this exercise difficult to do by yourself, look for a guided-relaxation CD. A couple you could try are *Guided Meditation: Six Essential Practices to Cultivate Love, Awareness, and Wisdom,* by Jack Kornfield, Ph.D.; and *Complete Relaxation,* by Denise Linn. Or you might try a stretch, meditation, or yoga class. You could even get a massage. The massage-therapy industry has exploded over the past few years. We're such a crazy, busy, out-of-touch society that we need to be pummeled, twisted, and soothed, which allows us to get release from our bottled-up inner feelings. Ever had a massage, and from out of the blue your eyes started to water? That's not the expression of your external feelings, but actually of *internal* feelings in your heart. The way into your mind and heart is through your bodily clues. Getting connected to them is the first step toward lowering your walls, the ones you didn't even "feel" you had.

Inquire

Gather more information about your behaviors. Be willing to listen to others' views and to ask yourself the hard questions. And here are some of them:

- When did this all begin?

- How often am I acting out this self-destructive behavior?

- How has this behavior changed over time?

- What have I gained from it?

- What have I lost from it?

Your answers to all these questions are pieces of a puzzle. By gaining access to them, you have a choice as to how you'll behave: whether you'll stay stagnant—and some people do—or do things differently than you have in the past.

Any kind of exploration with a view to understanding your Defenders must occur not only in an ongoing monologue with yourself, but even more important, within the context of relationships: with friends, a loved one, a therapist, or a group. Without these, you can't get serious insight into your Defenders. You need more than one person who will act as your mirror for your behaviors.

Notice

Search out when and where you engage in this behavior. What leads you to this self-destructive path? Notice thoughts, situations, and bodily clues that get stirred up at certain times, in particular places, or during specific events. A sure way to discern when and where these "trigger points" occur is to get yourself a small notebook and write them down. Once you have an actual written record of these triggers, you're able to look back over them and recognize the patterns. And an important step in breaking down those patterns that keep your heart walled up is to see them for what they are. If you don't care to put pen to paper in the conventional sense, send yourself an e-mail and keep a file on your computer. Start a blog for your eyes only or one that you can share just with trusted friends and family members who will give you feedback in the form of comments. This is perhaps the newest version of "candor contact"!

Experience

It's not the feelings that have been destroying you; it's how you've *discounted* them that's made you lifeless and unfulfilled. Take these feelings and experience them; bear them in a healthy way. Act to revitalize your feelings.

One method of doing so is to ignite your passion. So often when you deny *un*pleasant emotions, pleasant ones become a distant memory as well. By reacquainting yourself with joyful, positive feelings, you can withstand the not-so-good ones with less pain.

Many of us have forgotten or neglected those activities and interests that make our hearts pound and our spirits soar (some have never even uncovered them). When was the last time you got goose bumps? Remember what excited and engaged you as a kid, and discover ways to reexperience those things. Have a shot at a new activity that you've always wanted to try, do something physical every day even if it's just walking around the block, find a cause that you can get behind and throw yourself into it wholeheartedly, or get out and revel in nature.

A satisfying life—and it's a life accessible to all of us—isn't dependent upon any particular activity or skill level, but rather, your engagement in your chosen pursuit. When you find activities that make time fly and leave you excited and invigorated, you'll remember how that feels; and you'll be on your way to the richer, fuller times to come.

Pursuing passion takes courage, since it often means letting go of fears and situations you find comfortable. But consider what's more likely to provide those experiences of passion: what holds you back or what sets you free?

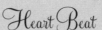

Heart Beat

When the National Consumers League and Harris Interactive recently conducted a poll of nearly 2,000 American adults, they found that 52 percent of those surveyed referred to themselves as overweight, and only 12 percent said they were obese. But based on the height and weight measurements they reported, the actual statistics show that more like 35 percent are overweight; and 34 percent are obese, severely obese, or morbidly obese. Since people tend to underreport their weight, the number is possibly even higher. These figures also conform more closely with data from the Centers for Disease Control and Prevention, which estimates that 33 percent of U.S. adults are overweight and 33 percent are obese.

Clearly, there's quite a discrepancy between people's actual weight and how they're willing to see themselves. It seems that many don't want to face the health consequences associated with being overweight. That's a whole lotta Denial!

The disturbing part is that a surprisingly large proportion of those who are overweight (45 percent) and obese (19 percent) reported never having discussed weight with their doctor. Since being obese or even slightly overweight can have long-term health ramifications—including type 2 diabetes, heart disease, increased risk for some cancers, and arthritis—facing up to your true weight and addressing it can make a difference in your quality of life well into the future.

Denial has become a part of our daily lingo. We bet you know someone who people whisper about, saying, "She's *so* in denial." Or perhaps you're familiar with that old cliché—much beloved by comedians and country-music singers—"She's the queen of denial." Or how about the famous quote attributed to Mark Twain: "Denial ain't just a river in Egypt"?

We all nod our heads in agreement when we hear things like this. How many times have *we* been down that river, too? Sometimes it's a very deliberate act. We know we're doing it, paddling as fast as we can so as not to capsize and drown. But more often than not, we don't even know we have the paddles in our hands—not until someone or something shakes us up. And that's what happened with our friend and colleague Donna.

Donna Does Denial

Donna is a great example of someone who walked around for a long time knowing that she was wearing a blindfold with respect to her current situation, but unwilling to remove it. A 35-year-old educational specialist, she was an accomplished, well-liked, and social woman. She viewed herself as strong and self-sufficient, but nevertheless yearned for a partner to make her life more complete. For as long as we'd known her, she'd been looking for Mr. Right.

So we were thrilled when Donna told us about Steven, the new man in her life. This was "it"! (At least that's what she hoped.) She recounted how they were having weekend adventures together and sharing exhilarating physical challenges that she'd never experienced before. She felt stronger and more competent than she had in years.

Over the next year, Donna began to complain that she wanted more than just "dating," and felt that the level of commitment between Steven and her wasn't getting any stronger. Watching friend after friend get married and become pregnant left her increasingly sullen and sad. We gently brought up the fact that we hadn't heard anything positive about the two of them in a while. Donna agreed with us that she was frustrated and worried. But she would always make excuses for Steven, talk herself out of her feelings, and shy away from admitting what she really wanted.

Her uncomfortable truth was that she couldn't face up to the fact that she knew Steven wasn't willing to go deeper in their relationship. Her blindfold, her Denial, kept her in a state of darkness.

About 14 months into the romance, Donna went on a business trip that took her away from home for more than a month. On her own, she visited schools all across the nation. One evening she called us to talk about an epiphany she'd had on the road: She could make it on her own; she could be independent. She didn't need Steven, but she wanted him and the feeling of being a committed couple more than ever.

Once home, and knowing more about what she wanted for herself, Donna asked Steven where the relationship was going. When he remained noncommittal, she persisted, she pushed, she cried, and he eventually acquiesced. They became engaged. And Donna's ring blinded us all.

A few months later as she shared her wedding plans with us, we noticed that Donna's usually open, happy demeanor had become downcast and lackluster. Although the ceremony was only six weeks away, Donna wasn't attending to herself. When we asked her about the dress, the flowers, the music—the whole setup of the occasion—not only was she not into it, she was completely detached from it. This gave us great cause to worry. Donna's Defender of the Heart—Denial—seemed to be in full swing, and it was taking a toll on her mood.

We wondered what she was refusing to acknowledge. Could it be that deep down, Donna knew that Steven wasn't invested in this union? We hoped not, but nothing else made sense to us. Over the next few weeks, we tried to meet her for coffee, but Donna made excuses not to see us. We were worried about her but tried not to push.

In a message to us, Donna alluded to the fact that the couple's sessions with their pastor had been upsetting. She was learning things about Steven's entrenched rigidity toward childrearing and religion that she had not been privy to before. She relayed that it felt to her and to the pastor that there was no room for negotiating anything in this marriage.

Three days before the wedding and after a final session with their pastor, Donna's sister, Leslie, called to inform us that Donna had called off the wedding. She assured us that her sister had lots of family support and was doing okay.

A few weeks later, Donna asked to meet us in her office. Wishing we'd brought some coffee cake to sweeten the meeting (because we always bring food to a funeral!), we were surprised to find that she looked pretty darn good. Donna had had a very tough time of it, starting with halting the wedding "train" and all 220 guests who had been expected to attend. But she also let us in on how she'd come to grips with slipping out of Denial and into a reality check. Her fear of loneliness and her falling in love with the idea of marriage had eclipsed her concerns about the man.

At the time they met with the pastor, she admitted that she'd felt sick of living alone, she'd wanted to please her parents, and her biological clock had been ticking away. All these fears were stifling her openness to what she was really experiencing—a partner she wasn't meshing with. When the pastor said to the couple point-blank, "I'm very concerned about marrying you two," deep down his words felt so right to her.

"Candor contact" seeped through to Donna's inner struggles. Given her colleagues' concerns, her pastor's worries, and her friends' feedback that she wasn't acting like herself, Donna had the "Aha!" moment. All that blunt contact coming at her like a hail of bullets resulted in her removing her Denial blindfold. Up to this point, she'd been stubbornly refusing to own up to what was happening within her.

Although coming to grips with her Defender of the Heart—Denial—caused Donna sadness and resulted in the loss of a dream, it also set her on a course. She paid greater attention to her fears and learned from them. Instead of jumping blindly into her next relationship, she's now consciously and deliberately soul-searching, deciding on what she really wants in a partnership. Her desires are the same as they've always been: to have a family life. However, she's clear that she'll never get into a relationship with someone just to avoid being alone.

By now you should have a pretty good idea whether or not Denial is your Defender of the Heart. But just in case you're still in doubt, let's end with a little list that will make you laugh . . . or cringe when you recognize yourself!

You Know You're in Denial When . . .

. . . you were born during the Kennedy administration and you still shop in the juniors' department.

. . . you don't know how much credit-card debt you've racked up because you don't open the bills. (And in any case, you "only" shop the sales.)

. . . you had unprotected sex because someone that cute couldn't *possibly* have a communicable disease.

. . . you don't worry about the calories you take in just finishing off the kids' leftovers (because, of course, they don't count).

. . . you think people don't know how much you drink because you hide the bottles so well—in your desk drawer.

. . . you believe all that evidence is purely circumstantial: she'd *never* do a thing like that to you.

. . . you just know he'll change his mind about having kids after you're married.

. . . you wear a comb-over.

The Payoff

Denying that there's a problem, no matter what it is, can close you off from change, from growth, and ultimately, from getting what you want or need to make your life better. After you've done the exercises in this chapter, you'll begin to recognize just how you use Denial and will start to realize what you've been missing. Becoming aware is empowering, but it's only a start. Now you need to have the courage to take action.

Staring down the bogeyman won't make all your fear and pain evaporate, but every one of us yearns for a more meaningful life, and sometimes it takes being prepared to endure some discomfort if it also means we're open to feeling pleasure. Further, acknowledging your pain will allow you to seek comfort; owning up to your anger will help you find an appropriate outlet for it.

So give yourself permission to feel . . . genuinely and intensely. Experiencing the full scope of your emotions—dread, resentment, sorrow, love, delight, ecstasy—facilitates your coming to know yourself better and achieving greater intimacy with others. Imagine having relationships that go beyond superficial interactions and that are rich with communication, empathy, and potential.

Why would you want to *deny* yourself all that?

Chapter Two

Defuse Your Weapons of Mass *Projection*

Defendapedia

Pro·jec·tion (*pro-JEK-shun*): Attributing your own unacceptable, shocking, or embarrassing thoughts, feelings, and impulses to someone else in order to relieve your anxiety about them.

The place where we've conducted our therapy practice for years—the land of make-believe—is a city that you love to hate and sometimes hate yourself for loving. Los Angeles is a company town, and its entertainment industry dominates our popular culture. While it can enthrall, captivate, and amuse, it also has that dark and seamy side we're all too familiar with from the tabloids. It seems that most of the population can't get through the day without their fix of TV and Internet bulletins about the shenanigans of young Hollywood stars.

On a daily basis, we have names you'd recognize from the world of entertainment coming through our doors—actors, writers, and directors—as well as the below-the-line people (as they're called in the business), all those workers who make the movies come alive. One thing we can tell you for sure is that the glamorous, famous, and wealthy are no more immune to Defenders of the Heart than you are. In fact, this industry nicely lends itself to illustrating our next Defender: *Projection.*

Movie projectors beam light rays and film print onto a wide screen. A whole story plays out in front of you. And like the movie projector, you too beam your own light and inner print onto your life's screen. Your feelings—your internal world—are enacted before your eyes. By "internal world," we mean your motives, thoughts, and feelings—both wanted and unwanted—all those parts of you that live inside your conscious and unconscious mind.

As you are the movie projector of your own life, people around you, both intimates and mere acquaintances, become the screen for your projections. They then turn into the unknowing recipients of those parts of yourself that you just can't tolerate. And subsequently, you interact with them as if they do indeed possess those unwelcome characteristics you've dismissed from yourself. In order to help you rid yourself of these unwanted motives and impulses, Projection has come to the rescue. It, like all Defenders, is a way of making sure that your conscious awareness is protected from negative, anxiety-producing feelings.

If the movie-screen analogy doesn't work for you, another graphic way to envision this unique Defender is to picture a garbage pail. Imagine that you need others to be the receptacle for the emotional refuse you can't even bring yourself to acknowledge within yourself. You use *them* to dump all *your* garbage into.

We very clearly see this Defender at work in couples. Your garbage-pail partner is stunned by accusations, criticism, or blame. Often he or she will say, "Are you kidding me? What are you talking about? Are we in the same marriage here?" Your partner doesn't even know where you're coming from. This "garbage" from you is shocking to him or her. Why? Because it's usually a Projection of something within yourself.

This Defender of the Heart is so insidious that it can ruin marriages faster than a meddling mother-in-law! Our insight into just how menacing this Defender can be has proven useful when we've conducted our marital seminars. With Projection in the forefront of our minds, we've helped couples get a better handle on what their own garbage is and what is their partners'.

We like to start out all of our seminars with a very elementary but profound worksheet that we've found to be fun and eye-opening even for the most sophisticated communicators. For many years we had used a "face" feelings chart for kids we dealt with in therapy. We'd throw a big poster up on the wall with about 30 cartoon faces that represented myriad emotional states. You may have seen these in family-medicine and pediatric offices. We found out that kids aren't the only ones who have a hard time labeling what they're feeling. So we decided to use a feelings-chart handout for individual adults and couples. To our surprise, this simple device became a springboard for helping them get out of their heads and into their *hearts*.

Taking it to the next level, our use of the chart evolved into measuring how in or out of sync couples are with one another. Partners first check off how many feeling states they've typically experienced within the last six months. Then they look at the chart again and check off the feelings they believe their significant others had been going through over the same period. The last step in this exercise is to sit face-to-face and compare and contrast these worksheets. What is mind-boggling is how each partner often attributes feelings and states of mind to the other person that have very little to do with him or her. Interestingly enough, this opened up a way for us to grab hold of that amorphous Defender of the Heart, Projection, and explore its impact on a marriage.

Try this face exercise at home. If you don't have a partner, doing it alone will still be very informative. Pick out how many feeling states you experienced during the past week. You'll quickly identify a few that you easily recognize in yourself, but what is most invaluable and revealing is that you'll also connect to some that you weren't conscious of. These hidden feelings were very likely the ones you were projecting onto others.

Faultfinding

Another powerful and liberating exercise that we find helpful when working with couples is our fault-finding exercise. This tool works perfectly with Projection, as it amplifies the core tenets of this universal Defender. It's a clear way of "concretizing"—giving form to—this Defender that remains hazy, slippery, and difficult to grasp.

Remember the days when your mom would say, "It's not nice to point fingers at people"? Well, Momma was right. Her reasoning was that someday someone would point a finger back at you and your feelings would be hurt. But Mom didn't tell you that inherently when you point a finger—and finding flaws, imperfections, and weaknesses in others is certainly one way of doing so—there are always three fingers pointing back at *you*.

Try the following exercise for yourself. It's always prudent to do it alone, just you and your notebook. The truth of the matter is that it has more to do with you and your clarity about yourself than with your partner.

**The more insight you have into yourself,
the less weight your Projections bear on you.**

In your mind, point your finger at your partner (or friend, sibling, parent, or colleague), and ask yourself the following:

- What faults about this person bug me the most?

- How does he or she demonstrate these shortcomings?

- How does that make me feel?

- Do any of these faults resonate with me?
  What three fingers are pointing back at me?

Looking at You Looking at Me

The two preceding exercises turned out to be really helpful for Cindy and her husband, Jack, who came to one of our marriage seminars not long ago. Having been married for 12 years, they were looking for some tools to reawaken their passion for one another. They probably weren't expecting that getting a handle on this particular Defender of the Heart would be the key.

Cindy was a 43-year-old office manager at a major insurance company. She was a spunky, athletic person who always had something kind to say about everyone. Her idea of dealing with life was to be constantly on the go, on her cell phone with her girlfriends, and over-extended with community activities.

When Cindy met PR man Jack, it had been love at first sight. However, it was five years before they tied the knot. Jack, 45, being the more subdued of the two, was sometimes hard to read. They were jogging partners, but it was apparent that his heart was really into staying home, hanging out, and going to poker nights with the boys. Their different styles never seemed to get in their way, and over the years they learned to tolerate and appreciate their differences. Ever since they'd been in their 20s, it was evident to everyone, including Jack and Cindy themselves, that they danced to the beats of different drummers. But that had never gotten in the way of their romantic/sexual life. Back then, they were dancing the "horizontal cha-cha-cha" with great ease!

When Cindy was 34, she and Jack were ready to have the baby they'd been talking about for years. Organized and methodical, she had this baby journey all mapped out (or so she thought): she'd get pregnant that year, have the child at that perfect age of 35, and take the summer off work. Jack was on board. As was Cindy's style, she approached the making of a baby with great enthusiasm and anticipation, letting the whole world know what was to come.

After about a year and a half with no baby, some of Cindy and Jack's sparkle was diminishing. They went to see a fertility specialist with high hopes. But after six years, thousands and thousands of dollars spent, and too many disappointing heartaches to count, the couple made a conscious decision to stop the process of trying to have a child. They both were unable to wrap their heads around the idea of adoption, but together were resolute that their lives could still be meaningful and happy without a baby.

About a year later, Cindy and Jack signed up for our seminar focusing on couples who have been married more than ten years and are invested in keeping their marriages alive and vital. It covered questions of sex, communication, finances, children, and "Where do we go from here?" when a couple has been together that long.

Although Jack and Cindy came to our group with the primary intention of spicing up their sex life, the face tool was quite revealing. Not only did it uncover feelings that had been buried, but it also shed light on what was now making it difficult to get into the rhythm of that old "cha-cha-cha."

Both Cindy and Jack had been through hell over the past few years; the decision not to have a child had left them with deep scars. Although they were united in their acceptance of being a child-free couple, it was to be expected that some profound individual feelings remained.

We handed out the face charts and divided the participants into intimate groups of two or three couples. Cindy and Jack began to talk about feelings they thought they'd already expressed and worked out, as well as those they were unacquainted with and had kept buried inside. What surfaced within the confines of this exercise was both fascinating and scary. Cindy had been feeling that since their baby decision, Jack had grown colder and more distant, as well as more irritable, mean, and critical. She felt that her husband didn't love her the way he used to. She believed that she had remained the same toward him.

Then, using our faultfinding tool, Cindy reflected on the faults she'd found within Jack. She saw him as uninterested in sex with her, not as affectionate, and less available to engage in conversation.

Reflecting on her own three fingers pointing back at her, she asked herself: *Do any of these faults have anything to do with how I feel about myself?* And she had to answer honestly: *Yes.* Cindy began to search inside herself for the faults she found in Jack. She asked herself: *Am I cold? Am I distant? Am I irritable? Am I critical? Am I unlovable?* Answering yes to each of these questions motivated Cindy to pose the next one: *How am I demonstrating this toward Jack?*

Cindy was stunned and embarrassed as she gained clarity. What she had been experiencing as coming from her husband was mostly originating within herself. Much of it was *her* "garbage." Although Jack was visibly saddened and disappointed about their struggle with infertility and the financial toll it had taken on their lives, Cindy hadn't been aware of the enormous emotional toll it had taken on *her.*

Cindy felt betrayed by her body. Seeing Jack as more distant and less available to love her was actually a reflection of her deep belief that she must have been unlovable. After all, didn't she fail as a woman, as a nurturing partner, by not being able to give the two of them a baby? Being such a capable person, Cindy had allowed herself no room for failure. Her unexplored self-criticism and self-loathing had taken up residence in Jack's world— or so she believed. Her Projection played itself out in her thinking that he was guilty of everything that *she* had been guilty of feeling about herself all along. True, Jack was quieter and more subdued than his usual self; he had been going through his own grieving process. But, in fact, he'd had a hard time connecting with Cindy because she'd been pulling away from him. She'd been protecting him from her internal critic and her "unlovable self."

Jack had become the screen upon which Cindy could cast those harsh critical feelings about herself in order not to have to look at them. He became her garbage pail.

True to form, as she tempered her Projection, their marriage got back on a healthy track. Although they'd been through years of pain and disappointment during the excruciating process of trying to have a child, they came out of it stronger and more committed to one another.

We know that you must be a gutsy person if you're willing to explore and take ownership of the unsavory feelings and thoughts that live within you. We also know that without self-exploration—the journey of developing insight into yourself—life just can't be that fulfilling. It's ironic. In the pursuit of a better existence, a more meaningful time on Earth, you have to come face-to-face with the darkest parts of yourself. That's the beauty of reclaiming your Projections. By taking back and owning those feelings that you've dumped onto others with great conviction, you now have the opportunity to understand yourself better. And in doing so, you're more likely to make the choices that help you grow.

Heart Beat

A study published in *Health Psychology* found that women who exercised for 20 minutes in front of a mirror felt less energized, less relaxed, and less positive and upbeat than those who did so without a mirror. These women also reported that they were more physically exhausted at the end of their workouts. So if people experience these negative effects from their physical reflections, imagine how enervating it is to be constantly confronted with your own traits and qualities that you're unwilling to embrace and have projected onto others. Here, the reflection you see represents all the negative parts of yourself that you're putting into the "mirror," into the other person (although, in this case, it happens to be *you*).

The Artful Dodger

Speaking of reclaiming your Projections, a young man we saw some years ago comes to mind. Art, 38, a very talented guy, exemplified his name in the work he did: every day he took a blank movie set and made "art" out of it! He was sought after by many studios and directors to design sets for big film productions. Although he'd been doing this work for about ten years and had made a tremendous amount of money, Art never felt successful.

About three weeks into a major new production, with the director breathing down his neck, demanding changes, Art was having some very weird physical problems. Never before had he experienced anything like the red bumps that were appearing on his hands and fingers. Thinking he was allergic to something, he carefully made a list of all the materials he'd come into contact with during the past few weeks. With his list in hand, he went to his dermatologist for a diagnosis. After several weeks of allergy testing and various medications, nothing relieved the rash. The dermatologist spoke to Art about the possibility that something else was going on. Had he been under a lot of stress? Had he been dealing with things that were unsettling for him? In other words, had he considered the possibility that these physical symptoms were reactions to the stress and strain he'd been under?

With a sneer, Art dismissed the doctor's expert advice and went to the "top" dermatologist in Beverly Hills for a second opinion. Art was *really* ticked off when the second doctor handed him our business card.

Meeting Art for the first time was *not* one of the highlights of our week, yet it was quite memorable. He came in very tightly wound up and treated us like he was doing us a favor by gracing us with his presence. Cautiously and gently, we set out to understand this guy. He relayed to us what was happening with the new director on the film he was working on and the angst he felt in having to kowtow to this man's ever-changing mind. Although Art told us that the business was filled with critical, temperamental, cold, and demanding people, this director took the cake.

We were curious, as we are with everybody, about Art's life and who he was in his world. We learned that he'd been single since the end of a serious four-year relationship in his late 20s. Since that time, he hadn't been dating much. He was an avid tennis player who spent all his weekends on the courts or watching matches. He had a group of tennis buddies but told us that they didn't socialize off the court. Art had a brother and a stepsister, neither of whom he was close to, and although his dad and stepmom lived only miles away, he rarely saw them. Art's mom had passed away when he was in his teens.

Work consumed most of Art's time. We found it interesting that an auspicious beginning got him into set design. He spent his college years at MIT, graduating with honors in engineering. One of his professors had been moonlighting as the director of a summer Shakespeare play at a very small off-off-Broadway theater— *way* off! He told his class that there were summer jobs working backstage, and Art decided to sign up. That was the catalyst that would change the course of his professional life forever.

We marveled that a guy with a degree from MIT would make such a bold 180-degree turn. He agreed that it was the craziest thing he'd ever done, but spoke of it with very little pride in himself and his accomplishments. He appeared dismissive of our admiration. He did tell us how as a kid he'd loved painting and building things but had never finished anything. When we questioned him further, Art laughed bitterly and said he always found that his "tinkering" wasn't good enough to complete. Ironically, Art became great at a line of work that demanded timely completion of projects according to deadlines dictated by others.

We asked him why he hadn't pursued studying the arts when entering college. In his home, it had just been assumed that you couldn't make money or have long-term job security with a creative career. After all, his father had been the CFO of a company he'd retired from after 35 years.

Even though Art had achieved much success over a long period of time, he still believed that his dad wasn't happy or proud of him. On the contrary, for many years Art had felt criticized and put down. Yes, his father had been skeptical of this career move back in the day, and he'd made it clear what he wanted for his son. However, Art was still holding a grudge against him. Although he told us that his parents had funded his move to Los Angeles years before to start his career and were first in line to see his movies, he couldn't even give them any credit for that.

What's more, we were struck by our sense that Art had a grudge against *us*—that we weren't good enough either. Art was finding fault, and we were feeling it. He was critical of any suggestions we offered, he questioned us about our credentials, and he never stopped harping on how horrible he found the parking in our building. Right before our eyes, we were seeing a man who had mastered the skill of highlighting other people's slipups. Art found fault with the dermatologist, his parents, the entire entertainment industry, and now with us. *Hello!* If this doesn't equal Projection, then we don't know what does.

A fact about Projections is that there is usually a grain of truth to them. Art's dad *was* a critical parent who had his own agenda regarding what was and was not acceptable for his children. He'd shown his displeasure and been unsupportive at a time when his young son needed more than he could give. Art may have been justified in feeling misunderstood, and was subsequently angered by his parents' missteps. But what he did along his journey to adulthood was to take those critical parts fostered in him by his parents, believe them wholeheartedly, and transfer them onto the world at large. How could he not? He learned from the best. His dad was a world-class projector in his own right. Perhaps he, too, had been on the receiving end of criticism from a parent who'd never found what he did to be good enough. After all, the apple doesn't fall far from the tree!

While it's true that we all need to be reminded just how powerful and influential our parents are in the development of our feelings about ourselves, Projections don't always grow out of a critical mom or an unloving father; sometimes they originate from within *us*. Remember, the Projections we use are born of shame, embarrassment, and discomfort about feelings, impulses, and thoughts that we're terrified of owning. Regardless of the origin, as adults we must all take responsibility for becoming conscious of how our early experiences impacted us.

For Art, those critical messages and the pressure he put on himself to do everything to perfection created a toxic wasteland for him and those around him. He was inhabited by an internal bully, and he couldn't bear it. His self-hatred and feelings of imperfection were too ugly for him to confront. Subsequently, in order to believe he had goodness and value, Art had to rid himself of those feelings telling him how awful he must be. What he "cleverly" did was to shove those critical, unwanted parts of himself onto others around him. "I'm not awful . . . *you* are!" *Phew!* He was able to get away from those demanding critics. Or so he thought. Now the critics were not only still inside him, but outside him, too.

Until Art learned, with our help, that *he* was the one who felt "not good enough," he would forever be stuck in Projection hell. *We* had certainly been the recipients of his hell, his critical Projections.

In the end, we were able to help Art understand that when he met the director he was now working with, he'd found an even stronger, more unforgiving perfectionist. This was the final straw. Art couldn't stand this guy's cold, harsh, mean, and unavailable nature—it was too close to his own style. Unaware of how demeaned he felt in this bully's presence, Art had to rely on his body to tell him that it was too much. Although he had to be brought kicking and screaming into awareness of his perfectionistic, critical attitude, he was at last able to come face-to-face with his beliefs about himself.

For as long as Art remembered, he'd never felt good enough. He recognized that he felt he would never measure up to the man whose unconditional love he had craved so urgently. This conviction had led him to view those around him through a prism of Projection. Seeing that, he better understood how he had been living a life of constantly putting upon others what he had so desperately run from in himself.

Our way of helping Art become cognizant of what he was doing and feeling was to first and foremost set up a supportive, nonjudgmental place—one that was not the least bit reminiscent of his own mind. With his insight into how his Projections had colored his behavior and how his internal critic had left him distant and isolated from those around him, Art was able to calm down, listen to others more, and be less judgmental toward himself. The offshoot was that his body, too, calmed down, and in turn, the rash disappeared.

Pinpointing Your Pesky Projections

So we know where Art's Projections came from. Now let's find out about *yours*.

One of the most helpful ways to develop greater insight into yourself is to become aware of how you think about others.

Although this Defender is easier to identify within the confines of a relationship, it's helpful to begin the journey of tackling your own pesky Projections alone. Pull out that notebook again and answer the following questions:

- What repetitive negative thoughts and feelings about others keep coming up in your life? (If you're unable to produce a list, reread Chapter 1!) For example, more often than not do you see your co-workers as lazy? Do you view your bank teller as an idiot? Do you find other parents in your neighborhood to be incapable of disciplining their kids?

- Have you heard these same things said about *you* before? If so, when was the first time?

- Do you think any of those negative statements could have had more to do with the person who said them than with you?

- If you haven't heard these things from others, where do you think they came from? Do you remember a time in your life when you called yourself lazy, an idiot, or a bad parent?

Read through what you've written. If you've been candid with yourself, you'll begin to make out themes— what you project onto others time and time again. By seeing these clearly, you've already taken strides toward reducing their hold over your life.

The next thing you need to do in order to get a grip on this elusive Defender is to grow more compassionate toward yourself. When you lack insight and are out of touch with how you really think and feel about yourself, it's easier to live your life by becoming hateful and taking out your own resentment on others. Therefore, it's imperative that you begin to develop compassion for yourself. In the absence of this self-directed tenderness, Projection is, without a doubt, your weapon.

Positive Self-Talk

So how do you develop this insight, which will eventually marginalize your Projections? The first step is to cultivate *empathy:* being able to understand and identify with others' feelings. And how you talk to yourself (your self-affirmations) is a major factor in doing that. The words and statements you use over and over make a huge impact on your view of yourself and the world.

When we've asked patients to write down their perceived strengths and limitations, we're always surprised by how quickly a long list of negative traits surfaces. Even more surprising, it's like pulling teeth to get people to come up with positive ones.

The power of those critical words and negative assessments wreak havoc on your psyche. That disparaging view of yourself can only lead to unforgiving and uncomplimentary ideas about others. And you don't even realize it! It's critical that you find a way *not* to be critical! Being kinder to yourself will take away the sting of attacking others with your own self-disgust, and your faultfinding will diminish.

So here's how to get out of your own way: make a list of your negative and positive qualities, and then ask yourself these questions:

- What are the five traits I like best about myself?

- What are the five traits I like least about myself?

- How much time do I spend each day focusing on these attributes?

- Do I spend more time on the negative or the positive?

Positive self-talk is about turning lemons into lemonade. Or, put another way, it's all about reframing: taking something harsh and turning it around. So now, look at your negative traits and see how you can reframe them. For example:

Negative Self-Talk: *I'm a big, fat pig.*
Positive Self-Talk: *I'm not exactly the weight I want to be, but I'm working on it; and in the meantime, I'm healthy.*

Negative Self-Talk: *I'm a moron because I was chicken and didn't take advantage of the real-estate boom.*

Positive Self-Talk: *I put my money in conservative mutual funds in order to feel comfortable. I'm glad about that.*

Negative Self-Talk: *I'm the worst parent for yelling at my kid in front of her friends.*

Positive Self-Talk: *Raising a teen is tough, and most of the time I pay attention to my voice and tone.*

Negative Self-Talk: *I'm disgusting for having sexual thoughts about my neighbor's husband.*

Positive Self-Talk: *He's an attractive man, and these are normal thoughts. I would never act on them.*

Stay aware. Listen to yourself; catch those negative, destructive patterns of thinking; and replace them with more upbeat, optimistic, constructive, and affirmative beliefs. Positive self-talk quiets disapproving chatter, and self-encouragement helps you feel more secure and diminishes the power of your Defenders.

Finally, don't ever tell yourself anything that you wouldn't tolerate someone else saying to you. We know that's easier said than done, but fake it till it feels real for you. Make sure your internal dialogue is positive, and be gentle with yourself. We always tell our patients: "Be the kind of mother to yourself you'd like to have." Now that you get the gist of how positive self-talk works and have a better handle on what's been so ingrained and automatic for such a long time, you'll be amazed to find that you no longer define others in the same negative ways.

Still not sure if Projection is your Defender? Perhaps the following will clear it up for you. (Just to warn you, some of these examples might be uncomfortable to confront.)

You Know You've Discovered Weapons of Mass Projection When . . .

. . . you believe that everyone cheats on their taxes because you do.

. . . you know road rage is all about those *other* idiots speeding and driving badly.

. . . you force him to break up with you when you're the one who really wants the relationship to end.

. . . you say, "He despises me," when actually *you* despise you.

. . . you're jealous because *you* love her, so everyone else must be attracted to her, too.

. . . you're having an affair and everything your spouse does seems suspicious to you.

. . . you think everything in the media is disgusting because it's so loaded with sexual innuendo.

The Payoff

Projections seem to relieve you of personal responsibility. In the process, they also prevent you from seeing what you really need and then taking charge and moving forward in your life.

It's exhausting to be constantly at odds with those around you because you're hurling your criticisms and

judgments onto them. Keeping up that barrage of negative self-talk is, likewise, tiring. In addition, when you
stop confounding your loved ones by dumping your
garbage on them and finding fault with them, you can
turn them into your allies rather than your adversaries.
It only makes sense that your heart doesn't need to be
so heavily defended when you've got an army of friends,
family members, colleagues, and others on your side.
Throw in your newfound compassion for yourself and
you've now got a support system that will allow you to
let your guard down enough to face your uncomfortable
thoughts and feelings and deal with them.

When this Defender of the Heart lays down its
sword, all that energy will be freed up for other more
life-affirming pursuits, including your job, relationships,
creativity, passions, and spirituality.

Chapter Three

Quit Making Excuses: Reduce *Rationalization*

<u>Defendapedia</u>

Ra·tio·nal·i·za·tion (*rash-uh-nl-uh-ZEY-shuhn*): Dealing with disappointment, fury, or hurt feelings over an unbearable situation by covering them up with convoluted, self-serving, and often seemingly logical excuses.

Parenting is a relentless task, yet the rewards are unbelievable. The joy of watching children grow into fine men and women is, for many, the best reason to slog through the day. But helping kids go through babyhood, pass into adolescence, and finally reach young adulthood can often—let's be honest—also be brutal.

Besides being parents ourselves, we've been running parenting seminars for many years. Moms and dads come into our groups with high hopes, often dreaming of "the right advice" that will get them out of a stalemate with their children. Sometimes we help them, and their relationship with their kids takes a turn for the better. Sometimes they need more help than we can give them in the group, and we recommend that they come in to see us for more private work. Occasionally we're as flummoxed as they are! Frequently in these groups we see the frustration and embarrassment that occurs when parents recognize that they haven't been connecting with their kids with patience and forethought. We can almost predict that a couple of times in every group, we'll hear at least a few parents justifying the actions they've taken—or perhaps *haven't* taken.

And that brings us to our next Defender of the Heart: *Rationalization.* Nowhere is this Defender used more by the parents of adolescents than on the subject of our current societal attitudes toward sex . . . what a surprise!

In a recent group filled with parents of seventh and eighth graders, one of the mothers noted how she found her daughter watching a commercial for a new TV show for teens. The characters were kissing openmouthed on a bed while undressing each other . . . at 7 o'clock in the evening, no less! Another dad chimed in, commenting that the songs his son listened to in his room had lyrics all about sex and large buttocks. Yikes! The discussion turned heated, even though all the parents agreed that life had been different when they were kids and that now there are so many more opportunities for exposure to sexual stimuli in popular culture.

We zeroed in on the goal of setting healthy limits around sexuality. Just as we predicted, a few people began to justify why it was too difficult and too time-consuming to even try to establish any boundaries in their homes. Some of the parents' reasoning sounded just like their kids':

- "All of their friends are watching these shows."

- "Everyone they know listens to the same music on *their* iPods."

- "They're going to have sex whether we like it or not."

These immature statements allowed the parents a way to avoid their discomfort. First, being a limit-setting parent would remove them from the realm of being their child's best friend and thrust them headlong into the role of being a responsible guardian. That is certainly a tough and thankless job, especially with a teenager. Second, sexuality is a loaded topic for both parents and kids. Dealing with a child's emerging sexuality can stir up a multitude of emotions.

This is a time when parents tend to fall back on those immature Rationalizations because they *feel* a lot safer than the minefield they'd have to navigate if they met the issue head-on. And that's the operative word . . . *feel*.

Like every Defender of the Heart, Rationalization is a clever device we use to rid ourselves of disturbing thoughts and feelings. Rationalization leads us to a place where our uncomfortable sensations are systematically placed in an objective, nonthreatening space.

Rationalization flourishes during the most vulnerable of times. This Defender of the Heart pops up predominantly when you have to retreat from:

- Hurt and loss

- The disappointment of goals that eluded you

- Embarrassment or humiliation

- Feeling inadequate to deal with the situation at hand

Saying "You have to" sounds as if it's something you think about and make a conscious decision to do. But once again, remember that as in all Defenders of the Heart, the "have to's" often come from a very deep place—your unconscious—and you're not really mindful of them. Everyone sometimes calls upon Rationalization to get out of an emotional jam. Being human means that you're going to occasionally use this Defender knowingly—those are the times when you make excuses while some little voice inside your head is screaming, *Bull*&%!* It also means that in times of discomfort you'll spew out excuses or "rational" statements that even you believe—ones that you think *should* be true . . . but they're really not.

Heart Beat

A researcher at the University of Cincinnati's College of Business is studying "dirty work"—in other words, the kinds of jobs that have some type of stigma attached to them. He and his research partners are currently examining the role of managers in occupations such as prison guard, personal-injury lawyer, animal-control officer, exotic entertainer, and used-car salesperson. He's found that some managers adopt various coping tactics for dealing with the fact that they're in lines of work that the general public often shuns.

One way they do that is through Rationalization: they try to rationalize a difference between what they do and the work of their employees and peers. For example, the manager of a strip joint rationalized that he was separate from the sleazy goings-on at his club because, after all, he wasn't the one stripping. In another case, the manager of a commercial roofing company rationalized that the work his company did involved more skill and craftsmanship than the job done by residential roofers. A true case of Rationalization at work!

You rationalize in three main scenarios:

1. When *something has been done to you* that you can't bring yourself to confront . . .

- You got passed over for that job you thought you should have.

- You didn't get picked for the cheerleading squad.

- Someone outbid you on the house you wanted so much.

- Your best girlfriend didn't choose you as her maid of honor.

2. When *you've done something to yourself* that's too embarrassing or tough to accept . . .

- You tripped over your shoelaces and fell down in the supermarket.

- You locked your keys in the car—again.

- You had to get up and go to the bathroom several times during a business meeting.

- You chose not to attend a friend's funeral.

- You bought an expensive car that you really couldn't afford.

3. When *you've done something to others* that you can't face taking responsibility for . . .

- You rear-ended someone at a stoplight.

- You cut in line at the movies.

- You stiffed the waiter by not leaving a big enough tip.

- You didn't invite your neighbor to join the community basketball league.

- You yelled at your kids when they didn't do their homework.

These examples are just a few of millions of things that might happen. In your head, you've probably made your own list of those times when something has been done to you, you've done something to yourself, or you've done something to someone else and couldn't deal with it.

In order to make sense of the hurt and injury you can't bear, you'll build excuses—ways of thinking—and believe them to be true.

When we feel shame, embarrassment, or awkwardness, a very clever part of the psyche gets activated. You know how everyone talks about the ego? What is it, really? In modern-day society, *ego* has many meanings: it could refer to one's self-esteem, an inflated sense of self-worth, or in philosophical terms, the self.

However, according to Sigmund Freud, the ego is the part of the mind that contains consciousness. It's said to operate on a reality principle, meaning it allows us to express our desires, drives, and morals in realistic and socially appropriate ways. The ego stands for reason and caution, and it develops with age.

There is another part of us, which Freud called the *superego,* that points fingers. It can be helpful in keeping us "legit," in check, and on point with our moral values. But when we do something we know we shouldn't be doing because it goes against our deep value system, the ego defends itself by making excuses to protect our sense of self—who we are. It does so by coming up with logical reasons that are acceptable to our moral compass. And it does this many times a day!

An Exercise in Exorcising Your Excuses

For one week, keep a running tab of how many excuses you make in a day. Make a list of:

- The excuses you make that are deliberate—the ones that make your mind scream *Bull!* the minute they come out of your mouth. You're intimately familiar with these Rationalizations.

- The excuses other people have told you that you use. These are the Rationalizations that make complete sense to you at first . . . until someone calls them for what they are: excuses!

Acquaint yourself with your list. How has this catalog of logical reasons and explanations served you up until now? What are the tough areas in your life that you don't want to face? What are the consequences you've been suffering by *not* facing them?

The story of Austin, a long-term patient of ours, might help you recognize this.

Missing Out on the Dream

Austin was a college sophomore who had been in a children's group we'd run years ago. This group was designed for kids in blended families. Over the years we kept in touch with him and his wonderful family. Since we'd first met Austin, we'd marveled that he knew so early on that he was going to attend the same university and join the same fraternity that his dad did. Even at age nine, he came into the group wearing an oversized sweatshirt from Dad's alma mater. Austin's half brother, Mike, six years older, was the first to join their father's fraternity. Austin talked with pride about how someday all of their names would be on the fraternity wall.

Each fall Austin put in his yearly phone call to us. We were always touched by his ability to keep in contact and were honored that we held a special place in his life. The year came when Austin would be eligible to pledge his dad's fraternity, and we expected to hear all about it during the call. Austin started out talking about how great school had been going so far. He mentioned his social network and all the fun parties he was attending. He told us about his roommates, his classes in biology, chemistry, and ancient civilization . . . everything but what we thought we'd hear. What was glaringly missing was any mention of the one thing he had always spoken of first and foremost: the fraternity. Being the kind of people who don't let anything pass us by (our strength *and* weakness!), we gingerly brought it up. We asked him about pledge week.

There was a slight hesitation. For someone like Austin who never hesitates, this blip was big enough to drive a Mack truck through. We sensed that something wasn't right. Austin flippantly dismissed our question by saying, "Those stupid idiots didn't make me a pledge offer." And then he went into great detail about how over the last year he'd come to realize that fraternities were really all a big joke. He was adamant that they were for the guys who didn't want to grow up and only wanted to "get wasted." After all, he continued, "I'm not in college

just to socialize. I'm in it to do something with my life."
He further explained that he'd never really admired or
trusted his dad's business partners who also had been
frat brothers.

For the past ten years, the fraternity, its brother-
hood, and its positive impact on his father's whole life
had been Austin's focus. Now all we were hearing about
was how relieved he was to have more time for his studies and how glad he was to meet nonfraternity guys, who
were much more interesting to be around. Knowing Austin, we thought his words just didn't jibe. We asked him
if he was *really* okay. He wouldn't go there with us. Also,
we knew that delving into how he really felt about this
calamity was no longer our role. He was clearly using
Rationalization to defend his heart from hurt. He hadn't
been asked to be part of something that had meant so
much to him, his brother, and his father for so long.

In Austin's case, missing out on the dream he'd held
since childhood was too painful for him to meet head-
on, so he threw up roadblocks to guard against those
excruciating feelings of loss. He shielded himself too
much with those Rationalizations, and they did him a
disservice. He was unable to make peace with his injured
heart and *really* move ahead in life.

When we stay in the mode of Rationalization for too
long and don't face the certainty of sorrow, more loss
and unhappiness is sure to follow. We all do it at some
time or another—we all find ways of dealing with standing in the middle of a crowd with egg on our face.

Austin needed to find another place to "roost." He
needed friends to hang with. It was essential that he
not remain stuck wanting something he would never
get. This was of paramount importance in order for him

to move on with his life. But he had skipped over the crucial step—to acknowledge and admit to himself and others the feelings that he was running from: hurt, disappointment, humiliation, and so on.

And there's the hard part. How do you make those submerged feelings come to the surface? *Lie!*

Listen, Interrupt, and Experience

To catch yourself rationalizing, try the following **L-I-E** exercise.

Listen

Pay attention to the words you say. Are you using typical Rationalization phrases? Common ones are:

- I don't care.
- It's no big deal.
- I didn't want it anyway.
- It's not my fault.
- It was never that important to me.
- I don't have any feelings about it.
- It has nothing to do with me.

Interrupt

When you hear yourself saying these statements out loud or to yourself, interrupt yourself and rethink them. Stopping yourself in "mid-think" seems as daunting as catching a butterfly without a net. But don't despair. The more you capture your pessimistic beliefs, the more familiar you'll be with your thinking and feeling patterns and the more effortless this will become. And what's the secret method you'll use to interrupt yourself and your Rationalizations? Turn your negative thinking on its ear! Restate the "truths" you've been using to delude yourself, transforming them into positive statements:

- I do care.
- It's a big deal.
- I really wanted it.
- I screwed up.
- This was very important to me.
- I'm really upset about what happened.
- It has everything to do with me.

Experience

Face your visceral reaction when you feel the loss or embarrassment. And each time you practice doing that, you learn to better examine and tolerate the feelings you're running from. Where in your body are you having a physical sensation? Does your face grow hot? Does your stomach get tight or nauseated? Does your heart race? Do your boobs hang low; do they wobble to and fro? (Okay, that last one was just some levity over a tough Defender to lasso!)

Using Rationalization is a guarantee you'll never be truly satisfied. It's a strategy for knocking down your hopes and dreams. What you really want out of

your life will go unnoticed. Rationalizing is a way to move on without realizing what you're moving on *from*, without considering what you're losing. And in reality, you won't be moving on at all.

For Austin, not paying attention to what he hungered for cost him dearly. He was already isolated and left out of his father and brother's fraternity, and his rationalizing surely perpetuated this loss. Rationalization devalued his relationship with important people in his life. When he kept his heart guarded from his pain, he was saying, "I don't need that closeness with my father and brother. It's no big deal to me." And ultimately, he was destined to act as if that were true. This "lie" would maintain his aloneness and shield his heart from his real desire: attachment. Ironically, if he could have lowered his guard and exposed his true feelings to himself and his loved ones, chances are, he would have solidified his place in the "fraternity" of his family.

If Austin's story hasn't clarified the concept of Rationalization for you once and for all, our quiz might do the trick. Answer the questions quickly and from your gut. Don't try to figure out the "right" response.

Let's Say That . . .

1. Your best friend tells you, "You look like you've gained a few pounds since we last saw each other." Would you be more inclined to say:

a.   I just bought this outfit; it must make me look fat.

b. Yeah, I've been stressed out and eating for
    comfort. I need to get back on a healthy plan.

2. The young woman in the next cubicle got the
promotion you deserved. Would you be more inclined
to say:

a. She must be sleeping with the boss. And any-
    way, I didn't want to work those long hours.

b. I feel that this is unfair. I need to talk to my
    supervisor.

3. The bank called you again because you bounced
three more checks. Would you be more inclined to say:

a. I'm closing this account because this keeps
    happening at *your* bank.

b. I'm mortified. I forgot to deposit two checks,
    and I'll take care of it immediately.

4. Your neighbor calls to complain that your dog has
been barking all morning. Would you be more inclined
to say:

a. All dogs bark! And if you don't like dogs, you
    moved into the wrong neighborhood.

b. I'm so sorry he woke you. I'll keep him in
    the house in the mornings.

5. Your doctor told you that your blood pressure is
way too high. Would you be more inclined to say:

a. Traffic was awful this morning, and there's
    never any place to park in your lot. Anyone's
    blood pressure would be high.

b. I'm worried about that. I need to make some lifestyle changes and find a way to deal with stress.

6. You accidentally deleted some vital data from the company computer. Would you be more inclined to say:

a. I told them months ago that we needed a new system.

b. I feel terrible about all this. I'll work over the weekend to re-input it.

If you primarily answered *a*, it's likely that Rationalization is your Defender of the Heart. You can clearly see how you have a tendency to jump on any lame excuse rather than face feelings such as embarrassment or fear. Do this often enough and it becomes your habitual style of thinking. You push away genuine feelings and maintain a lock on your heart. Hanging on to this Defender will certainly not help pinpoint what is vital for you to experience greater satisfaction.

If you mostly answered *b*, you're ready to explore some more Defenders!

The Payoff

Rationalization puts your heart in a straitjacket. Set it free! The pain you feel over missing out on something that you wanted will be short-lived. But by running away from it, you lose the chance to have clarity on what's most important in your life.

What you wanted *was* truly important, so don't pretend that it wasn't. When you rationalize your goals away, you're failing to recognize what they mean to you. This may cut you off from true satisfaction. Having an appreciation for your desires even when you don't attain them helps you direct your energy positively toward other dreams that you *can* reach. The longing is a real and valuable thing, a passion that can motivate you. Instead of negating it, find a different way to nurture and satisfy it. When you stop fooling yourself about how badly you wanted something, you'll connect with something else that's just as meaningful—and you'll go for it. You'll ultimately find that fulfillment comes in many different forms.

Chapter Four

Use Your Head and Your Heart: Inhibit *Intellectualization*

Defendapedia

In·tel·lec·tu·al·i·za·tion (*in-tl-ek-choo-uhl-uh-ZEY-shuhn*): Using words, definitions, and/or theoretical ideas to explain away emotions associated with painful, uncomfortable events or thoughts.

Ever had a conversation with someone and observed that the deadpan way the other person told you the facts just didn't jibe with what should have been the emotional impact of the story? Listening to him or her, *you* were the one undergoing flurries of sadness, worry, or distress in your heart, while the speaker seemed seriously disconnected. You were the one left "holding" the intensity of the situation.

What you've witnessed firsthand is a flight from mindfulness, from aliveness. Your companion was retreating from being susceptible to real anguish. At the same time, he or she was freezing out the possibility of real contact with you.

Our next Defender of the Heart, *Intellectualization,* does that to a person. Many mental-health professionals talk about this as an "isolation of affect," by which they mean that your manner—your demeanor—is removed from the emotional content of a situation. We like to call it "silencing your heart sounds." Intellectualization is all about that place in which one part of your being is cut away: the essence, the soul, the longing . . . the *you.*

This Defender is deceptively user-friendly when we're touched by serious illness. In today's world, what really grabs us by the "heart" and puts the fear of God in us is cancer, the "big C." How many times have you been to a dinner party and the topic turned to who had just been stricken with some form of this disease? Have you heard of anyone relaying so-and-so's cholesterol level to the table? Doubtful! But cancer has taken center stage in many of our lives, and knowledge and awareness about this equal-opportunity aggressor has grown exponentially. And that's a good thing, especially for early prevention and treatment. The statistical rates of survival are increasing, and the truth is that cancer is often no longer a death sentence. More survivors than ever are around to tell their tales and educate others.

But as important as the accumulation of data is to improving survival rates, that very same information is often called upon to help remove emotion from a searing emotional experience. Facts, figures, recent polls, front-page news articles, and Internet postings become the shields we throw up to guard from the fear, pain, and overwhelming anxieties that are stirred up when we're faced with the uncertainties of life. And so this Defender of the Heart is invoked, rushing in and safeguarding our fragile sense of self.

Armed with the latest cogent reports, Intellectual-ization becomes the buddy that helps you disconnect from *pain* (your feelings) and align with the *brain* (your intellect). In the cancer scenario, how understandable it would be to shy away from the frightening, panicky feelings that would engulf you if your doctor delivered that dreaded diagnosis. Remember, your Defenders of the Heart are there for a purpose. You're not reading this book to strip yourself completely of those comforting ways. Rather, you're searching for patterns within yourself that might not be of service in the long run. Although it makes sense that you might grasp on to facts and scientific jargon that would, for the moment, release you from your dread, this can also do you a disservice.

This Defender represents the "thinking" person's bag of tricks that you use to rid yourself of the fears of so many things you face—not just cancer. Intellectualiza-tion is the path you go down to numb yourself emotion-ally while at the same time creating a sense of control. In this turbulent world in which you're at the mercy of machines, strangers, and medications that you can't even pronounce, giving up that intellectual control appears at first to be too great a loss. And no one should ask that of you until you're ready. But once you *are* ready to let go of the grip you have maintained on logical information, good things occur.

When you stop using all that you know in your head as a way to shelter yourself from what scares you most—falling apart—you are actually *less* likely to feel like collapsing with fear. Lowering your Defender, that removed stance from your emotions, allows you to explore other avenues of support.

Letting down her Intellectualization Defender led our patient Susan to feel more comforted and in control of her own medical condition.

She Said, He Bled

It was Susan's second time around battling cancer. She was just hitting the five-year mark where she thought she could breathe easier. After all, doesn't it state in the journals that if you're in remission for five years or more, the possibility of recurrence greatly diminishes? But, unfortunately the breast cancer was back again. And with a vengeance: it was now at stage IV, which was two levels worse than when her doctor first diagnosed it. James, Susan's husband, was terrified and called us. He brought all the fears of the past five years into our therapy room.

James and Susan, both 52, had been high school sweethearts and had been married more than 25 years. Off and on over the past two decades, they had visited us individually, together, and sometimes with their kids. As Susan liked to say, "We love to come in for our tune-ups." They were the kind of people you love to have grace your office. They were smart, funny, compassionate, and kind to one another and their children. They had been able to take advantage of our assistance over the years during crises and heartaches, exhibiting respect and an ability to listen to what we said and make it even more meaningful in their life together.

One thing that became more clear to them over the years—and this couple laughingly pointed to it often—was their compatible but very different styles when dealing with tough times. James knew now that this would be one of those occasions where their differences might leave both of them feeling alone and disconnected. Already Susan's computer had been getting more time with her than he and the kids had.

Susan, a very warm and loving person, had always been someone who found solace in the written word. An only child, she had an inquisitive mind, and her relationship with her widowed father was based on debate and intellectual banter. Susan's mom had died of breast cancer at age 48 after she had suffered for three years. Susan had followed in her father's footsteps and become the family research scientist. Letting Dad in on how scared she was had often led to his withdrawal, but hunching over medical journals and library books kept him near and dear.

When James entered Susan's life at 15, he brought his family with him. His sisters and brother were open to her immediately, and she felt like she'd found a new home. The family was loud, boisterous, and oftentimes argumentative; and no one could accuse them of being "buttoned up." And Susan was in heaven. As with any two people who are trying to forge a life together, the very thing that she loved about James and his upbringing—his desire to bring emotions right out in the open, his ability to be unguarded—often became a thorn in their sides.

Years later when Susan's cancer recurred, James was frightened. He needed help in sorting through what *he* was afraid of losing versus what he needed to do in order to help *her*. It was her body, her cancer, her life—James felt shut out. Each time he approached his wife to talk and share his emotions, fears, and concerns, she focused her attention on facts, figures, statistics, and new treatments. She even began talking of going to Mexico for alternative therapies.

History had shown him that this was Susan's way of coping. When emotions had been too hot to handle, Intellectualization was the way that had offered her contact with her father. She'd completely shut herself off from the comfort James and the kids could give, and he was having a difficult time remembering that this was where she would go in times of extreme pain. He was astounded by his anger toward her and needed our help to feel compassion both for himself and for her.

This cancer was bigger than all of them. Susan just didn't have the time to come in to see her "old" therapists. At least with James in the room, we could support him and be a sounding board for speculation about the family's future. Knowing Susan so well, we told him that helping her reduce the choke hold of Intellectualization would help him and the kids, too. It was critical that James reduce his frustration and begin to feel that he wasn't impotent.

We encouraged him to use e-mail as much as possible to connect with Susan. Also, he could find articles on his own and devise pros and cons about alternative treatments. Everyone in the family would pitch in with information gleaned from a lot of sources.

We needed James to get his foot in the door first and foremost. It was imperative that he align with Susan in the only way she could be reached at this time—through words, not feelings yet. To strip away her Defender right now would leave her too raw too soon.

At the same time, to honor the importance of James's need to reach out with warmth and concern, he would continue to write her love letters and send tender e-mails and flowers when he felt the urge. He would have no expectations of receiving the same warmth and love from her. By his matching up to her needs, she would become less guarded, more able to face her fears, which would ultimately allow them to comfort one another.

Over the years, Susan had the luxury of an occasional safe haven in which to check in: her long-term therapy relationship with us. We'd provided a place where she was able to come to an understanding of the familial roots of her Intellectualization. By gathering the history of how she'd developed this particular Defender of the Heart, she'd been able to get something of a grasp on it; she'd been able to see it, acknowledge it, and break through it more than once in her life. Despite this, she still resorted to her favorite Defender in times of extreme anxiety.

Although the next six months were filled with angst and pain, James's ability to nurture Susan with what she needed at the time helped her feel supported, understood, and cared for. Slowly, she was able to come to her husband not only with her medical apprehensions but also with her fear of dying and leaving her loved ones. As she did so, she and James became a team again. They began to laugh and cry about what had been their world and their hopes for their life to come. Susan even came back to *us,* and we all cried together.

Sometimes Intellectualization is so embedded into every facet of your life that it *becomes* you—how you represent yourself in the world, your personality, your style. You must know a few people who always portray themselves as one big mound of gray matter. They're smart as a whip yet dumb as a doorknob when it comes to matters of the heart. They're what we usually call "out of touch," unable or unwilling to be moved by joy, loss, or sorrow.

Sadly, there's a physical condition that equates to being immune to feeling anything. It's a heartbreaking disorder—*familial dysautonomia* (FD)—that mostly affects a percentage of Ashkenazi Jews (Jews with ancestry from Eastern Europe). FD is a disease that causes the autonomic and sensory nervous systems to malfunction and affects the ability to feel pain. When people struggling with this meet with bodily injury, they feel little or no physical sensations. They can't make tears and are oblivious to being hurt.

Are you thinking that it might be great not to feel pain? Certainly discomfort is no fun, but both physically and psychologically it gives us signs that we need to attend to something. Think about putting your hand on a stove and only knowing you were in trouble if you smelled the flesh burning! Intellectualization is a way of having *emotional* dysautonomia. Imagine if you lost your dog of 16 years and didn't feel anything. That would mean that those years together had made very little impact on your heart.

**Only when you know sadness can you
know happiness. Pain and suffering are
a good indication that you're alive. They keep**

**you out of harm's way and allow you to be
grateful for the quality times in your life.**

You may not have the advantage of someone being
by your side to bore into your Intellectualization like
Susan did. Of course, as with any Defender, seeing yourself and your escape mechanisms up front without someone to bounce everything off of is difficult. This book
will stand in for another person to help you think and
reflect at this moment. Being honest about how you use
highfalutin words or phrases in the pursuit of protecting
yourself from emotional harm is a tough road to take. It
requires a willingness to grapple with how far removed
from yourself you really are, as well as a readiness to be
vulnerable.

Why would you even go there, knowing that you'd
need to examine your Defender of the Heart? Most
times it takes an event in your world that shakes you
to the core. Something happens to you or a loved one,
and your usual way of responding doesn't work for you
or the other person anymore. If you're someone who
resorts to Intellectualization, chances are that others are
fed up with your habit of distancing yourself from them;
and you, in turn, are wondering why you feel so alone.

The following steps will assist you in evaluating
whether Intellectualization is your Defender of choice.

Got Brain?

Get out of your head and into your heart! Pull out
your journal and do the following **B-R-A-I-N** activities.

Be Brutally Honest

Over the past year, what events have occurred that were out of the ordinary for you? Come up with at least three. It could be a death, a breakup, a job change, a health scare, financial struggles, an argument with a close pal, a move, or an embarrassing situation. Don't gloss over anything, no matter how trivial you think it is. These things don't necessarily have to be negative. They could also involve events that should have provided joy and excitement, emotions that you didn't feel. Say, for example, you got some type of accolade at work, and instead of being proud and happy, you justified it with facts and figures.

Review

Review your reactions to these events. Rather than allowing yourself to feel upset, angry, hurt, stressed, or ecstatic—as the circumstances may have called for—did you find yourself "numbing out" by spending hours searching the Internet for answers? Did you attach yourself to CNN, the library, or newspapers and magazines? Were you on the hunt to find information that would help you make sense of an out-of-the-ordinary incident instead of perhaps crying on a friend's shoulder or expressing your fears to someone who cared and who would be sympathetic? In an uncomfortable tête-à-tête with that friend, colleague, or partner, did you find yourself pulling out facts and jargon to secure your position, to preserve your stance, rather than expressing your feelings of disappointment or annoyance? Instead of throwing yourself a party in celebration of exciting news, did you simply move on to the next job at hand?

Assess

Assess the emotional impact. Chances are, your intellect was working overtime. To even ask someone who intellectualizes to assess emotions is like asking them to scour the desert for water. But try to get in touch with yourself from the neck down. Maybe you can recall some physical sensations that you experienced at the time of the event. Do you remember a racing heart? A headache? A hot flush across your cheeks? Dizzy feelings? Back pain? A queasy stomach? Constipation or diarrhea? *Any* bodily sensations at all? If not, you really are highly married to this Defender!

Now consider the other ways you could have reacted to the situation: With tears and sadness? With hurt and anger? With fear and frustration? With jubilation and delight?

Intrude

Break your pattern of being in your own head by intruding inside someone else's! Who are some people you admire who don't act as you do during hard times, who amaze you with an ability to allow themselves to be impacted by their emotions? It could be a relative who calls all members of the family to talk when she's upset, a business associate who takes the entire department out for a celebratory lunch when he makes a big sale, a good friend who cries upon hearing how a hurricane or tornado destroyed a town, or an acquaintance who is well known for making a funny story out of his embarrassing *faux pas*. How might they react emotionally if they were confronted with one of *your* out-of-the-ordinary situations? Most likely not how *you* have been doing so. The very way they express their feelings without using gobbledygook or patronizing others with their know-how is probably what you hold in high regard and maybe even envy. *They* are willing to be affected by their lives . . . *you* can do it, too.

Nurture New Behaviors

You gotta fake it till you make it. Practice pretending in private that you, too, would react to something differently. You've sliced away so much of yourself for so long that it might be hard to even think of yourself as someone who could react emotionally.

You can try renting sad movies or documentaries about some subject that enrages and moves you, such as racism or the Holocaust. Watch them by yourself and allow the feelings to well up.

Crank up your emotions by doing something physical that's safe but challenging and engenders feelings of fear—rock climbing, for instance, or hang gliding—or that are exhilarating, such as running outdoors, biking, or dancing.

There's another great way to stir up your emotionally flavorless pot. On the radio shows we've been involved with, people who called in often "intellectualized" themselves and everyone else right into a deep sleep! To shake them up from their underlying depression due to being so removed and detached, we'd ask them to step outside themselves and help someone or something else.

If you go down to a homeless shelter to slop some food onto a hungry guy's plate, if you walk the dog for someone who's housebound, if you sing Christmas carols a few weeks each year at an Alzheimer's unit or bring toys to kids on an oncology floor, some part of you is bound to be awakened. And Intellectualization doesn't mean a thing to someone with dementia, an animal, or a little kid . . . so they won't let you get away with it! Find some place you can bear to be and just do it.

Heart Beat

Young children view violent events in emotional terms, while older ones see violence in a more intellectual way. This is according to researchers at The Ohio State University who surveyed 5th, 7th, 9th, and 12th graders three weeks after the Columbine High School shootings in 1999 and while NATO was in the midst of bombing Serbia. The younger children seemed to be more personally affected by the violence, putting a human face on the events and using language such as *hate, anger,* and *fear.* They also seemed concerned with the emotions of both the perpetrators and the victims.

The older children, on the other hand, gave a more analytical account. They differentiated between the motives behind the NATO bombings and the Columbine shootings and made a distinction between the causes of the two incidents. They seemed quite detached from the events.

The researchers concluded that older children—and, by extension, adults—may be less emotionally upset than young kids about violence around them, and that when we intellectualize violence, we're not always attentive to the human consequences.

So now you're pretty clear that this Defender of the Heart is not an easy one to get a grip on. If you mostly resort to your intellect, you might hold it in such high regard that your feelings hardly ever show themselves. Our patient Marcus was a king at cutting himself off from his emotional world.

Big Talker

At 35, Marcus had logged years in which he hadn't paid much attention to his personal emotional music—joyful or painful—that resonated inside. Silencing his heart sounds, hushing those feelings that made up the notes in his songbook, had become his *modus operandi.* Early on, Marcus became a pro at using Intellectualization to distance himself from hurts and disappointments. He just carried on, calling it up unawares in times of conflict or frustration.

Marcus was a big guy. He had always been the tallest kid in grade school, always the biggest and strongest guy in high school. Being popular and smart was his job, and he handled it well. He was his school's best fullback on the football team and had played first string on varsity since he was a sophomore. Although he had been focused and his entire family had lived and breathed this sport, he was also a kid who'd been taught to use all his gifts and not get too pumped up with himself. His dad, also a big man, struggled with diabetes and had lost his eyesight a few years before Marcus got a full athletic scholarship to a major university. Nonetheless, his folks hardly missed a high school game, and they were there at many of his college ones as well.

It turned out that Marcus wasn't as successful at university ball as he had hoped. He never really broke through, and in his junior year he lost his scholarship. He was mortified. The world had always pictured him as a jock. His family rallied around him like they always had, and Marcus pushed through the heartache. He was a good student and had other skills to fall back on. As a kid, he'd seen his father bounce back after his blindness. Marcus was in awe of his dad and how he'd had a continuing life of productivity despite experiencing a life-altering trauma.

There was little time for grousing about unsavory predicaments in his home. The way the family joined in to set him on a new path was admirable. Everyone put on their thinking caps. Information was gathered on what kinds of jobs were available in their hometown and what sort of work Marcus could succeed at. Not much was said about the loss of football, and life went on.

Thirteen years later, Marcus and his wife, Tricia, came to our grief group after Tricia's father died suddenly. Marcus was now a high school chemistry teacher and the father of a toddler, with another baby on the way. We learned that, surprisingly, Marcus had turned away from physical exercise and playing sports and had concentrated on working his "mind muscle." He was no longer just a big guy—he was fat, and wasn't interested in changing that circumstance. He'd become a voracious reader and was often the one who could draw a crowd around him—not watching him play ball this time, but rather listening to him pontificate. Marcus never came off like a know-it-all, but he did have a mind that seemed to spit out minute details and complex lingo with the best of them. Teaching was a good career for him, and he was happy.

But the fact that he was overweight, actually obese, worried his wife and mother quite a bit. His dad had died young—at 61—of complications from diabetes, and Tricia was so scared that Marcus, too, would die early. It seemed that she had not only come to our group for her own sake, but also with the hope that somehow being so close to grief and death would touch Marcus and get him to change his ways.

During one of the Saturday-morning groups, Tricia directly brought up her dad's sudden death and how unfair it was that a man in such good shape, even at age 72, should go without warning. Her pain began to turn toward Marcus, and she started to raise her voice at him when she told him of her concern about *his* health.

Someone in the group remarked that Tricia seemed so angry that day. She sheepishly acknowledged her anger and became more subdued and in touch with her sadness. She told Marcus, "At least you still have a chance to lose some weight and turn your life around." We noticed that the more Tricia became alert to her feelings and implored Marcus to hear both her sorrows and her fears, the more he "silenced" his heart.

Marcus's body seemed to sink deeper into the chair, and he appeared to withdraw. We observed that he began to speak in a passionate-sounding way, but what he spouted off about was theoretical, devoid of feelings. He went off on a tangent, recounting the studies on the newest fat-busting pills and how unhealthy and damaging they could be. He shot out statistics about how people who diet regain the weight and then some, and how research indicates that yo-yo dieting can have profound negative effects on the heart.

The group was spellbound, and even we got caught up in the lesson. But every one of us in that room was on some level experiencing the feelings that Marcus was bypassing. We were sad, worried, angry, and concerned. So where were *his* emotions throughout this entire well-informed tirade? He wasn't on his high horse, and his intellectualizing wasn't meant to be cruel or dismissive, even to Tricia. But it was as if he was missing the big picture. He was circumventing both his and Tricia's genuine need for support. Rather than dealing with his feelings of loss and his wife's fear that he would die because of his obesity, he fell back on familiar ways. He resorted to nullifying any feelings that had been stirred up, especially when it came to loss.

Tricia asked us to meet with both of them after the group. She was grieving over her dad's death and was desperate for Marcus to be there for her emotionally. She felt so alone and was surprised by her own intolerance toward him. The things that she'd accepted and sometimes even admired all these years—his calm and neutral manner—agitated her now and left her feeling isolated and wanting to lash out at him.

We surmised that Intellectualization had been Marcus's "drug" of choice for many years. Tricia was the one who relayed to us the losses her husband has suffered—his football career and scholarship, his dad, and his own healthy and active body. Marcus chimed in with information about these distressing situations. But even that day as he revisited these painful places, it was apparent that he met them with "brain power," empty of feelings. It was clear to us that the more Marcus felt weak and powerless, the more his mind would grab on to a device to aid him in bolstering himself up. His tactic was to hold fast to facts, statistics, and information and run away, unconscious of his feelings, which were tagging along behind.

Marcus, who was really a good guy, was touched by Tricia's tears. He wanted to do right by her, although he didn't have a clue what to do. He admitted that he'd always handled life in this way and was proud of that. However, now his Intellectualization was distancing him not only from himself but also from the one he loved the most.

We supported Marcus by letting him know that we all use our Defenders of the Heart to shield ourselves from feelings of terrible despair. While they protect us, they also keep us from connecting to those people who mean the most to us. We suggested that Marcus start to lower this Defender but pointed out that he didn't have to lose it completely. We said this to him because we know something about "intellectualizers."

People who are entrenched in Intellectualization are walled off, detached from feelings—even more so than people who tend to use other Defenders. They silence their heart sounds so well that their feelings are completely dormant, and reaching in to awaken them must be done slowly and cautiously. We sent Marcus home with our B-R-A-I-N exercise to work on. If in the process he wanted to share any of it with Tricia, that would be fine, but this exercise was strictly personal. We were sure that doing it and not having to let down his guard when he wasn't ready would have a positive effect on how he related to Tricia's needs. Ultimately, we knew, this could only aid Marcus in enriching his own life.

Removing the *emotion* from an emotional experience is the stuff this Defender of the Heart is made of. Reasoning yourself out of a sticky and often uncomfortable or anxiety-

**ridden issue is your way of blocking what
your unconscious feels is too hot to handle.**

Concealing Your Feelings

Intellectualization manifests itself in two ways. One
way is how Marcus did it, when you search out facts and
figures, information, and research that allow you to distance yourself from an emotional experience. The other
way is when you employ complex terminology or jargon
that throws up a barrier between the actual experience
and the feelings associated with it.

Here are just a few examples of common jargon
words or phrases we use to protect ourselves and deflect
the anxiety of a potentially emotionally "hot" subject:

- *My son was a victim of friendly fire.* (My child
  was killed by his own men.)

- *My grandfather expired.* (Poppa died.)

- *Her pregnancy wasn't viable.* (The fetus died.)

- *I was let go.* (I was fired.)

- *We're going to take a break.* (She dumped me.)

- *He has a great personality.* (I find him ugly.)

- *My father was a man of few words.* (My dad
  beat the crap out of me.)

We all use this intellectual gobbledygook at some time or another. Try coming up with your own list of phrases that you tend to use or that you've heard and can identify with. Chances are that it's not going to be easy, and it will be especially difficult if you're someone who so often resides inside your head and outside your heart.

If you're still struggling with this concept, do one more thing: see if you recognize yourself in the following.

You Might Be Using Intellectualization If . . .

. . . your friends tend to roll their eyes when you start talking.

. . . you've been called cold and logical.

. . . people describe you as a know-it-all.

. . . others come to you for information and knowledge rather than sympathy or comfort.

. . . you're usually the one keeping a level head when everyone else is running amok.

. . . you're drawn to professions such as professor, lawyer, or researcher but repelled by ones like nanny, creative artist, or therapist (!).

. . . you'd rather do public speaking than have a heart-to-heart conversation with one person.

. . . you feel out of place at gatherings of family or friends when everyone is "emoting."

The Payoff

Sometimes we're able to fool ourselves by coming up with intellectual arguments. Those words and explanations may sound good, but if we follow them, we're led away from reality and our true feelings.

Get better at paying attention to your genuine feelings and you'll be moving toward a more enriched life. Don't be half a person. Put both your heart and your head to work fully. When you don't use just your left brain and you stop dismissing how you feel, you'll open yourself up to others and their love and support.

Chapter Five

Laugh a Little, Cry a Little: Get a Handle on *Humor*

Defendapedia

Hu·mor (*HYOO-mer*): Using laughter or joking, especially sarcasm and irony, to get out of a jam or to soften feelings of anguish or discomfort in a given situation.

Eddie Murphy has been known to collect $35 million to write and star in movies. He's just one of our favorite clowns, along with Robin Williams, Will Ferrell, Steve Martin, Whoopi Goldberg, Chris Rock, Steve Carell, and many others. Their comedy resonates with familiar truths. We can relate to these people and feel that they understand us from the inside; they "get" us. We pay big money for wit, for slapstick, for anything that makes us chuckle.

Laughter helps us connect. Sharing a private joke, chortling over a funny movie, or exchanging conspiratorial grins in a crowd are some of the most intimate things we can do together. There's a lot of truth to the old saying that the shortest distance between two people is laughter.

Most of us will never make big bucks by being funny, but nonetheless the next Defender of the Heart, *Humor,* can enrich our lives in many ways. It's also a desirable quality in others. Ask any single person what characteristics they look for in a potential mate, and they will almost certainly list "sense of humor" high up there. Theoretically, finding a partner with this attribute shouldn't be a difficult task—after all, everyone has a funny bone, don't they? It would be comforting to think that even well-known killjoys like John Calvin and Attila the Hun found *something* to snicker about, as laughter is a universal (and exclusive) attribute of human beings. You might swear that your pet is laughing when he gets that silly doggy grin on his face and wags his tail. But he's just happy that you're paying attention to him. Only *people* laugh because they find something funny. Test it out: try telling Fluffy the one about the Pekinese, the poodle, and the rottweiler that go into a bar. . . .

So if laughter and Humor are such ubiquitous and desired human qualities, why have we made this a Defender? Well, it's no coincidence that many of your favorite comics have come from tough family backgrounds or have some kind of psychological concerns. Comedy can often serve as armor and as a very smart and sophisticated device that can remove your heart as far away as possible from feelings of unease, agitation, and pain. But there is a downside to this tactic. When you use it too often, it cuts down your ability to make your real needs and desires known. Instead of helping you connect, it isolates you.

And that's why Humor is the subject of this chapter. It actually can be a very clever, and often healthy, defense mechanism. Making yourself and others laugh and having fun isn't a bad way to go through life. In fact, it's really a good ambition. But it can come with a hidden cost if it's masking deeper emotions.

Humor can throw up a very acceptable, socially rewarding smoke screen that prevents you from seeing and feeling very real and important fires that may be burning inside. When that happens, you run the risk of not really living your life and not drawing the valuable lessons from the relationships and events within it. Humor, ironically, can then become a path to deadness, dissatisfaction, apathy, and depression.

Brad, a participant in one of our seminars, went down this path often.

You Must Be Kidding

Several years ago, Brad and his fiancée, Beth, came to one of our seminars on how to get the best out of a marriage. Brad was a highly paid comedy writer for television and the star of our class. He was funny, insightful, intelligent, and warm; and although he kept us all in stitches, Beth was by far his best audience. Throughout the ten weeks of class, the two of them seemed to have a close relationship. Still, we sensed that there was subtle underlying tension between them. And sure enough, months later we received a call from Beth. She told us that she and Brad were indeed terrific together—she admired and loved him deeply—but at times when she was sad, upset, or frustrated, she tended to withdraw from him. Brad didn't even seem to realize when she pulled away. She felt that he had tuned out not only when it came to her needs, but to his own as well.

When we met with them again, Beth told us that she'd been feeling aloof, isolated, and lonely for some time. We noticed that whenever she got emotional, particularly if she was sad and teary, Brad would call upon his quick wit. Perhaps he hoped to bring her around, but he was seemingly unaffected by her emotional state.

Zeroing in on Brad, we shared an observation: sometimes his Humor was a clever diversion from the feelings at hand. Every time it got "hot" in the room—whenever a feeling surfaced that Beth couldn't contain—Brad felt ill at ease. Unsure how to deal with that, he would reach into his abundant supply of jokes for a way out. Pretty quickly we had a hunch about what was cooking with Brad and the possible reasons he so often turned to Humor.

We know that so much about this Defender comes from ways of relating in childhood, and that Humor clearly becomes imprinted as a personality style throughout life because it's so rewarded. But before we made any further observations, we wanted Beth and Brad to get it for themselves. The following section lists some questions we asked them to ask of one another. The answers helped them on their journey toward illuminating what exactly was blocking them from feeling closer and happier.

You could work through these same questions with your closest friend. If you prefer to do the exercise by yourself, get out your trusty notebook and write down your responses. In either case, examine the insights you get from how you answer.

Role Playing

- Was your role in the family to be the smart aleck? The jokester? The household cutup?

- Why do you think this role was so needed in your family?

- Do you continue to play this part in your adult life?

- When do you call upon it in the present?

- Do you think this role enhances your adult life?

- Do you think it hinders you from developing close, mature relationships?

- Who were your role models growing up?

- Who are they now?

- Do friends and/or loved ones comment that your "role playing" isn't funny?

After going through the "Role Playing" exercise together in our office, it was crystal clear that Brad had learned his Humor Defender early on. When he was young and his parents were constantly fighting, he learned to make himself and others feel better by getting everyone to laugh. Doing so defused the household tension and reduced his internal angst. It made his world feel more secure, blocking out how upset and scared he'd become that his parents would divorce.

Now, however, Brad was being ruled by this Defender of the Heart. His Humor-based shield had become second nature. He realized from the preceding questions that when any tension or hurt feelings erupted, even if they bore no resemblance to those of his family, his knee-jerk reaction was to revert to his role of being the "king of comedy." His wit served a purpose, but sometimes actually made things worse.

Although it was Beth who had come in to see us because of her feelings of disconnect from the man she loved, actually it was Brad who discovered that his Humor was blocking his heart. He was the one who couldn't connect deeply with his fiancée because he'd been disconnected from *himself* for too long. Resorting so often to Humor meant he'd been missing out on a deeper relationship with the woman he loved. Due to his Defender of the Heart, both of them had been isolated, unable to lean on one another as they longed to do.

Over the next year, Brad began paying better attention to when and where he used his Humor. He was able to talk with Beth more often about his concerns. When he slowed down his quirky wit and let her in on his worries about his job, about being a father—about the deeper issues that kept him up at night—he experienced a sense of safety and comfort he'd never let himself feel before. It seemed that the more Brad acknowledged his humanness, the fuller his life became. He was able to use his Humor thoughtfully with loved ones . . . and, as a bonus, professionally he was soaring, too.

Recently Brad's favorite grandmother passed away. While at the grave site with Beth and his nieces, he joked about Grandma's feistiness and how any minute she was going to jump out and grab them. Thank goodness Brad's Humor was there to lighten the mood. However, when he looked into Beth's face, he saw sadness. At that moment, because of all the work he'd done, he was able to stop his joking, take a deep breath, hold her, and connect to his own true feelings—to his sorrow in missing his grandma. In a flash he realized how his Humor brought a little levity to the moment, but also kept him at a distance from Beth and her support and his love for her. Brad was able to ground himself, to be present in the moment, and to feel more connected with everyone he cared about. He had a choice now that he'd never had before: when and where to use his Defender of the Heart.

To keep that choice as fresh as possible, Brad went home that evening and got out his PalmPilot. He did the following exercise.

Calendaring the Event

Brad typed in the date of his grandmother's funeral and a word or two about how he felt at that time. Next year when that day came along, he would not only remember Grandma, but also be reminded that he had been in touch with a lot of feelings—sadness, joy, gratitude for Beth's support—that affected him at the moment.

Learning new skills and ways of being takes a lot of time and practice for everyone. All of us slip back into old patterns from time to time. By calendaring the event, it's a sure bet that you can conjure up the memory and be nudged into forward progress—a great way to avoid backsliding.

In your personal calendar or on your computer or PDA, plug in meaningful dates such as a loved one's funeral, birthdays, anniversaries, or personal moments that have great significance to you alone. When they pop up the next year, like Brad, you can hold on to your memory and have immediate access to a time when you lowered your Defenders.

Heart Beat

You've no doubt heard that laughter is the best medicine, and there's much truth to that. Scientists have known for some time that a really good belly laugh gives your system a workout. Your heart rate goes up, you're forced to take deep breaths, and your muscles become so relaxed that you can literally fall down or pee in your pants!

More recently, studies have found that laughing lowers blood pressure in people who are hypertensive and expands and enriches blood vessels. Further, this activity releases feel-good endorphins that leave you euphoric and can even bolster your immune system. So go ahead and enjoy a giggle, or revel in a full-blown gut-busting laugh—you'll feel great. And if you can find someone to share it with, so much the better. Humor, in its proper place, really is a healthy thing.

Humor is a wonderful tool for adapting to the stresses and strains of life. Although it's a defense mechanism, it's often a truly mature and constructive choice. But, like all Defenders of the Heart, it can sometimes generate a harmful result by distancing us from ourselves, from our loved ones, and from our greatest aspirations. Unfortunately, this is just what happened to Bobby.

A Lesson Waiting to Be Discovered

Bobby was one of the most playful, energetic women you could ever hope to meet. A fit 48-year-old redhead, she had been single for more than ten years. With no kids, she was the aunt everybody loved and the friend who would immediately be by your side in a pinch. Bobby was the first to arrive at every party and the last to leave. Always quick with her funny stories and dry, sarcastic wit, she was often the center of attention.

In her late 20s, Bobby had graduated with an MBA from a high-powered Ivy League business school. Her prestigious degree, coupled with her winning personality, had taken her career far beyond her early expectations. The women she went to school with were still her best friends, and all of them were big alumni supporters of the university. They often hosted local fund-raisers for their alma mater and even helped the school by interviewing candidates for their MBA program.

Bobby had been asked to be the keynote speaker at the yearly holiday faculty/student luncheon. She was thrilled and honored. Shortly after this invitation came a confidential call from the chairman of the business school. He told her that a board member was about to retire. If Bobby was available, the chairman assured her, she would be a perfect candidate to fill the post. And she *was* available, with bells on!

She began having conversations with a girlfriend already on the board about how exciting it would be when they worked together. They were both confident that the timing was terrific and that Bobby would be a shoo-in.

But as things turned out, the "shoe" didn't quite fit. One week before Bobby was to speak at the luncheon, she received a painful call from her friend. Several board members weren't thrilled with Bobby's outspoken political views. They happened to hold a majority and denied her the spot.

Despite the snub and the pain Bobby felt, she sat down to write the next week's speech for the very people who had just said "No thanks—you aren't what we want." Possessing an indomitable nature, she resorted to her ever-present Defender of the Heart: Humor. With it in high gear, Bobby peppered her speech with sarcasm and biting wit, perhaps more biting than even *she* realized.

The whole purpose of the luncheon was to let the graduating MBAs know how much the university hoped they would continue to support the institution after they'd launched their careers. The audience was also filled with successful board members, past and present. Bobby soon had the crowd laughing with her sardonic style. She cut down the board, skewering them one by one with her sly barbs. Her concluding statement, underlining how important it was to stay devoted and active with the alumni association, was filled with sour grapes. Looking straight at the president of the board, with a laugh Bobby declared, "Look where it got me!"

Bobby's Humor was usually a healthy and attractive part of her personality. However, her Defender of the Heart had often been a means of insulating herself from disappointment and sadness. Although Humor kept her troubled heart at bay, it also had a nasty way of preventing her from grasping her genuine wishes and desires. In this case, it drove an even deeper wedge between her and the university community she wanted to be part of.

Lots of smart and funny people use incisive jesting to keep their true needs hidden and protect themselves from feeling vulnerable.

Over the next few months, Bobby got back to her busy life. One day a call came from the local alumni chapter to say that they'd missed her at the last two meetings. Bobby knew that she'd been avoiding the meetings and was relieved that someone had noticed her absence and wanted her back. She then reflected that lately after work she had gone straight home, not heading to the gym like she used to, but rather going for a wine bottle instead. Part of her wanted to stay holed up, but a stronger place within her knew that something just wasn't right. One night while listening to the *Marilyn Kagan* radio show, Bobby decided to make an appointment and come in to see us.

Early in our first conversation, we noticed that our new patient automatically brought in her smarts and quick thinking to cover her hurt and her pain. Bobby kept us laughing right along with her. We asked her to reflect on what friends, loved ones, and colleagues would say about how she related to others when she was upset and disappointed. She came back with one emphatic word: "Humor!"

We gently pointed out how, even in the therapy room, her Humor was blocking her from making real contact with us and with herself concerning the pain she felt about the board seat. She quickly connected with how deeply injured she had been feeling. Shame-faced, she wondered out loud if this wasn't something she did a lot—using her smart mouth to get herself out of prickly situations.

Although Bobby had a very active life, there had been many times when her Defender of the Heart had kept her from feeling fulfilled. We asked her to tell us of occasions when she'd truly wanted something yet used her Humor to deny the strength of those desires. Through her tears, Bobby disclosed that the board seat represented something major to her. Being an active part of the board was her way of fulfilling her wish to leave a mark on the world and to make a personal contribution to the university that had done so much to shape her life. While many of her girlfriends had families and kids, the university had become her focus.

Bobby knew that her Humor had gotten her far. She was aware that winning people over with laughs was an easy and immediately gratifying thing to slip into. At our suggestion, she committed to spending a specific time every day journaling her experiences and feelings to help zero in on how her Humor might be a hindrance, not always a help. She answered the following questions:

- What happened?

- How did you use your Humor?

- Do you know what you were really feeling?

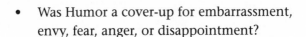

- Was Humor a cover-up for embarrassment, envy, fear, anger, or disappointment?

- Was your Humor used wisely and appropriately?

This helped Bobby keep track of how and when she fell back on her old Defender of the Heart.

Ask yourself the same questions. You'll begin to see when you use Humor in a positive way and when you misuse it, thereby preventing yourself from feeling real happiness.

Sharing This Awakening

We recommended that Bobby share her new insights with a close friend. This is a great way of keeping yourself accountable in the use of your Defenders. By broadcasting an epiphany, you own it and have the support and help from a trusted friend to keep your powerful new insight alive and fresh.

Bobby came to grips with the importance of what the board represented to her. Grieving this loss kept her from staying stuck in her negative Humor and walling herself off. She then had the room to be open to new opportunities and eventually became the head of a mentoring program for inner-city kids. Plus, she stayed active with her local alumni association, which kept her connected to her alma mater. Bobby remained very funny and was better able to understand her Humor. Simply making people laugh—unreservedly—became her joy now that she wasn't using Humor to block her heart.

You should be able to understand if Humor is your Defender, too, by now. But if you still need a clue, read this:

You Might Be Using Humor as a Defender If . . .

. . . you frequently hear yourself explaining, "It was just a joke!"

. . . you're the life of the party, but you're there without a date.

. . . being the class clown worked for you as a kid, so you're sticking with it now.

. . . you often make witty, self-deprecating remarks about your body, possessions, family, or achievements.

. . . you often make cutting, sarcastic remarks about *others'* bodies, possessions, families, or achievements.

. . . you tend to accuse people of having no sense of humor.

. . . you're pretty sure that if you didn't laugh, you'd cry.

. . . people turn to you when they're looking for fun, but not if they need help with a problem, solace, or a shoulder to cry on.

. . . *you* don't have a shoulder to cry on because everyone thinks you're always happy.

. . . people have told you that your smart-ass, sarcastic ways can be a turnoff.

The Payoff

It's better to feel the hurt, even to cry sometimes, than to cover up your feelings so much that you forget what they are. Is your laughter healing, or is it concealing? *Feel* the difference. Laughter, especially if you frame it around sarcasm and irony, can cloak the anguish or discomfort of a situation.

A little laughter *and* a few tears every day are good for the soul. Be comfortable with the full range of your emotions. And take a look at your Humor barometer. Is it in the red zone? Do you keep it on the sarcastic, ironic, self-deprecating, or hostile mark? Dial it back to a midrange setting. Very soon you'll develop a greater sensitivity toward your emotions and those of the people around you—helping you tune in to when you're covering things up rather than just having fun. And once that happens, you'll no longer be holding people at arm's length with your Humor.

Chapter Six

Rid Your Life of Hand-Me-Down Anger: Diminish *Displacement*

Defendapedia

Dis·place·ment (*dis-PLEYS-muhnt*): Diverting alarming, humiliating, or unpleasant feelings and impulses from one situation, object, or person to someone or something seemingly less threatening.

Thank heavens that dog is man's best friend. If this hairy, smelly, slobbery, gloriously warm bundle of devotion ever caught on to what was coming down the pike when his owner got home, Spot would be out the door in a heartbeat—unconditional love be damned. But the dog is always the last to know.

Spot is at the end of a chain of events set in motion by the bullying boss who ungraciously rips into his second in command because things weren't exactly to his wishes. The subordinate guy grins and bears the humiliation . . . or so it seems. He clamps his lips together to keep from ripping right back into his superior.

With an angry, burning sensation in his belly, Mr. Second-in-Command jumps into his hot little BMW. After driving 30 minutes—fueling his rage with loud hard-rock music and controversial talk radio—he reaches his new upscale suburban house with its huge mortgage. Mrs. Second-in-Command is anxiously waiting to tell her husband how her day went, but he has no patience for anything she's saying. He's still fuming about the previous encounter at work, so he gives her an earful for not picking up his dry cleaning.

She, in turn, gives him the cold shoulder, leaves him to fend for himself at the wine cabinet, and heads for the bedroom to call a friend. On her way there, she passes her 15-year-old son's room. She sticks her head into his messy space. Without warning, she goes on a rant about how she's told him a million times to clean the place up, and then grounds him from his best friend's party the next night. Turning her back on him, she warns him that he'd better walk Spot or he'll be sleeping outside *with* the damn dog. Furious, the son grabs the leash, drags the poor pooch outside, and proceeds to mindlessly and roughly walk him around the block.

Just like all the "Seconds," the dog simply wants a little loving! How stereotypical this is: man is ticked off, and the dog gets beaten. Stereotypes *become* stereotypes because they usually begin with some form of the truth. And the truth is that at one time or another, all of us have been caught in a position with our "pants down."

Haven't you been in situations where you've felt disgusted with someone, enraged by their treatment of you, and embarrassed for yourself? The conscious image you seek to put forward to the world has been compromised, trashed. When caught in this state of affairs, you may resort to a Defender of the Heart that helps preserve your sense of self: *Displacement.*

Angry, spiteful, painful feelings—too dangerous to act upon and too scary to understand in the moment—must be relegated elsewhere to protect your "fragile" ego. You seek sanctuary from situations that incite your negative feelings by attacking something or someone else whom you perceive as less intimidating. At the moment of your embarrassment, rage, or discomfort, you're cognizant of something happening to you that you didn't feel prior to the encounter: you're aware that you're seeing red.

Your feelings, jumbled and befuddled, have to land on something less threatening. No matter where you discharge these "hot" emotions, you never really experience a sense of satisfaction, a feeling that everything is all right. And to boot, you're now dealing with a new mess that you started by displacing some unpleasant emotions onto those in the line of fire. You feel guilty, rotten, sick to your stomach, remorseful, embarrassed, and more inadequate than before. And the toughest problem is that your initial internal angst remains somewhere within you.

Heart Beat

Displacement can often take the form of bullying. After all, what are bullies but those who take their own anger and frustration out on the most readily available target? While we tend to associate this behavior with schoolchildren, a recent survey revealed that 37 percent of American workers —around 54 million people—have been bullied in the workplace. Researchers at the University of Minnesota have shown that the people most likely to bully on the job are those who themselves feel bullied, and this can rapidly lead to a toxic atmosphere in which the bullying keeps trickling down.

This is a good template to illustrate how *your* hand-me-down anger can also infiltrate your family and social life.

Hand-Me-Down Anger

Here's an example of how Displacement can not only leave you unfulfilled, but also create new disasters to clean up.

All in the same day Grace was left feeling alone and isolated from her best friend, Holly, as well as mad at her closest sibling, Anne.

Over the past month, Grace had been brainstorming the logistics for Holly's holiday bash that was to be held at her friend's house. Grace had even helped create some clever invitations. A few days before the shindig, she phoned Holly to ask her opinion about whether she should wear her black cocktail dress or her silver one. With obvious awkwardness, Holly replied that she had assumed Grace knew that this was a private party and wasn't open to anyone who didn't work at her place of employment.

Ouch! Grace was shocked and hurt that she wasn't invited after all the work she'd done. With blood pounding in her ears, she stated that it was no big deal—she got it—and quickly hung up. Immediately, the phone rang again.

It was her sister Anne. Before Grace could get a word in, Anne was off and running about how she was so sick of going to her in-laws' formal Christmas party every year and just wished she could stay home. Grace, the blood still pounding in her ears, ripped into poor, clueless Anne. Sucker punched by her best friend, she now turned around and hammered into her sister. With a decided lack of "grace," Grace exploded, shouting that she wasn't interested in Anne and her foolish in-laws, that she couldn't care less about the stupid party that her sister hated going to anyway, and that Anne was lucky she had anyone to love her at all. Well, needless to say, Grace certainly didn't endear herself to someone who would have otherwise been open to helping her with her own misery!

Everyone does the Displacement boogie from time to time. Sometimes we can't process the feelings we have toward the original person quickly enough, so someone less formidable steps in to be our punching bag, and we just snap. Grace wasn't a person who resorted to this explosive stuff very often, but when she did, it left her floating out to sea for a time, cold and nauseous. Not only did she need to get a grip on her feelings about the situation with Holly and let them be known, but now she also had a repair job to do with good old sis due to her Displacement.

Displacement is exactly what its name implies. To *displace* something (in this case, feelings and actions) means to relocate it to another place, to shift the focus to another area. So what's suggested by employing this Defender of the Heart is pretty clear: you're forced from within to pack your emotional bags and behaviors and move them from one target or locale into different surroundings. Inside, you have a false sense that the new place will better meet your needs by being less filled with danger and despair!

You believe that you'll be putting yourself in harm's way if you stick around to go head-to-head with that six-foot-tall, pimply faced, angry jerk (even if in reality she's five feet one and all peaches and cream!). You experience yourself as a person in the "one down" position, so you relocate, you shift . . . you get the heck out of Dodge. But the angst you feel takes the hike with you, and someone else becomes the recipient of your anxiety—someone who just happens to be there at an inopportune time or who you feel in the depths of your soul will stand by you no matter what you do.

In Grace's case, her sister Anne fit the bill on both counts. With a boss, a good friend, or a lover, the stakes are higher because in your mind, the ties to them appear more fragile. These meaningful people are very powerful, and because they're so important to you, you can't jeopardize the connection. Fearing that your feelings will put it at risk, you run. These relationships provoke a sense of dependency in you—feelings of need and defenselessness—and that can be very disconcerting. To rely on others for your livelihood or safety or to support your view of yourself may hurl you into a precarious position.

The fact is, depending on people doesn't have to lock you into feeling impotent and small. To form a

dependence on others is actually a healthy human condition. It's the only way to make for a worthwhile and
satisfying life. Needing and supporting one another and
struggling through conflict is the only way to reach
for what ultimately is the healthiest form of union—
interdependence with others.

Grace needed to go back to Holly and speak her mind.
She might tell her friend that she was embarrassed. She'd
assumed that she was invited to the party and was also
hurt that Holly had taken advantage of her help without
making it crystal clear that it was a private event. Only if
she aired those feelings could her relationship with her
best friend be richer and closer.

An Unexamined Life

So let's return to Mr. Second-in-Command. Things
would have gone differently for the poor dog if Mr. S had
been a better master of his own emotional life. Imagine
what he might have been feeling when he was called on
the carpet by his bully boss. Most likely he was ashamed,
embarrassed, angry . . . even scared that his job might be
on the line—and along with it, his income, the BMW, the
house, and possibly his family. He had a right to these
emotions. Who wouldn't? It's what is *done* with those
feelings that determines the course of this Defender.
Mr. S has never allowed himself to pay close attention
to those feelings—hanging on to them and tolerating
the dis-ease of them—prior to turning them on innocent
bystanders.

We know that many people like this—that is, those
who live an unexamined life—tend to suffer the most.

Their lives at home, as well as in their professions, erode over time when they routinely use Displacement instead of keeping their feelings close to the vest in order to learn from them. The Mr. S's of the world are left with emptiness and with an inability to push beyond their insecurities. There may not be anyone who sticks around to love them, nurture them, and meet their emotional needs. Even if the dog and the wife hang on and continue to be on the receiving end of constant unfounded attacks, there is very little connection remaining . . . and eventually, there's no love *left* to be lost.

How to Examine Your Life

By now you know that Displacement is used primarily when you feel intimidated and unsafe or there is a possibility of losing face or endangering your job, money, or relationships. It's imperative that you dig down deep to analyze your reactions. Work through these questions.

1. What do you usually feel when you're caught off guard or confronted by someone in your life who speaks to you in a callous fashion? Identify which of the following emotions apply to you, or go back to Chapter 2 and look over the face chart to find more feelings.

- Ticked off
- Resentful
- Embarrassed
- Sad
- Criticized
- Controlled

2. When these feelings are elicited, what do you do?

- Sit silently
- Get up and leave
- Go get something to eat or drink
- Ignore the other person
- Shoot back a nasty comment
- Find someone else to talk with
- Pick on someone else (Displacement!)

3. What sensations do you have in your body when these feelings arise?

- Chest tightening up
- Nausea
- Throat closing up
- Face flushing
- Heart pounding wildly
- Ears burning
- Head throbbing

The more you understand and learn what led you to use Displacement in any given situation, the more it will become second nature to deal with feelings in the present, with integrity and maturity.

Slamming Sam Instead of Picking on Rick

Some years ago, 22-year-old Chloe called the producers of *The Marilyn Kagan Show*. She had seen a TV commercial asking young women to call in who wanted to get an advanced degree after four years of college. The program was about looking into the lives of those who were making the conscious choice to pursue careers that would put their baby-making years on hold.

Although Chloe wasn't chosen to be on the show, she made an impact on all of us. Here was a terrific, smart, and beautiful young woman who had beaten the odds. She'd been putting herself through a prestigious university without any financial help from her elderly parents, while confronting the continuing challenges of monitoring her type 1 diabetes. She would soon be applying to a handful of major medical schools and was sure to be accepted. With so much on her plate, Chloe recognized her need to come in for some therapy. It was a pleasure to have her in the room. Although she was a young woman who certainly made things happen, we also saw someone who struggled to reveal her needs to those closest to her.

After three months of talking to Chloe, assisting her through the trials and tribulations of her young life, we found out that she and her boyfriend of six months, Sam, would be moving in together within a few weeks. It was clear that the two were getting closer. Chloe had never felt like this about any other man she'd gone out with before. She was so comfortable that she described Sam as family.

Chloe was getting more and more deeply involved with Sam; however, the man who'd had the most impact on her life over the past two years remained her research professor in biochemistry, Dr. Rick. Chloe admired his mind—his ability to synthesize an overwhelming glut of material and make it come alive. He was the overseer of her senior research project, which would not only help her gain admission to medical school, but would also be published in medical journals, co-written with Dr.

Rick. Not only had he become Chloe's academic mentor, but in the last few years he and his wife had come to represent vital parental figures to her. Dr. Rick could be warm, charming, and helpful—but, as his wife would always point out, he could also be extremely testy and was often short-tempered.

During the past few months, Chloe had become delinquent in handing in her part of the research project. Dr. Rick expressed surprise that he even needed to ask her for her work. And truly, it *was* so out of character for her. What Chloe hadn't been telling Dr. Rick or Sam was that she hadn't been feeling as well as usual. Her diabetes had been out of whack, and she hadn't taken the time to check her insulin pump for some time. Between moving into her "nest" with Sam and wanting everything to be just perfect, Chloe was stressed and couldn't seem to keep up her normal intense pace. Not wanting to burden those she cared about—fearing they would see *her* as a burden—she was getting farther and farther behind and couldn't seem to catch up.

One day after a very important experiment wasn't run at the lab, Chloe showed up 30 minutes late to her appointment with her mentor. Dr. Rick let her have it. He had been asking for weeks if something was the matter, but Chloe had denied that anything was off-kilter. Frustrated, and worried for her future, he brusquely reminded her that if she didn't pick up the pace and get her act together, not only would their article be in jeopardy, but so would her future medical-school hopes.

Chloe fought back tears and assured Dr. Rick that she would get it together. Still not sharing her health crisis, she left quickly and headed toward the student union, where she saw Sam talking to a pretty female student she'd never met. Furious, Chloe grabbed his arm and dragged him away. Sam, embarrassed and ticked off, asked, "What the hell is the matter with you?"

Chloe accused him of sleeping with the girl, and she threatened to move out. Sam was stunned, assuring her that nothing was happening, but he was outraged that she would even think that of him.

Over the next few days, things were tense between them. In therapy, Chloe spoke of how humiliated she was by her own actions and said that she couldn't believe how juvenile her behavior had been. She even expressed the belief that Sam would be better off without her. And she thought that Dr. Rick, even though he could be a beast sometimes, had a greater chance of success with someone else.

We knew that we had our own research project to uncover here! Our job over the next few months would be twofold: (1) to help Chloe gain more insight into how her past had impacted her present, and (2) to give her some backbone when being attacked for her shortcomings by Dr. Rick.

Being the only child of elderly parents had left her feeling that she needed to care for them and fend for herself. Furthermore, dealing with juvenile diabetes had led her to believe that she'd be too burdensome for them. So she became the little girl—and then the young woman—who never complained, never asked for help, and always explored her medical and social options by herself. Her parents, warm and loving individuals, often remarked that Chloe was so independent and self-sufficient. They marveled that she never asked for anything or got into conflicts with anyone.

In therapy, we continued to help Chloe uncover a greater understanding and acceptance of herself, as well as the feelings of dependency she'd long stuffed "underground." However, all of us knew that there was an immediate need to straighten out the fallout from her Defender, Displacement. Sam had been the unwitting target of her conflict with Dr. Rick, and making amends was of paramount importance. It was also imperative that she let her boyfriend and her professor know what was really going on with her, both physically and emotionally. Not only did she have to face who she was and what she was dealing with, but it was also critical that she not run away from Dr. Rick and the work they'd started.

Chloe acknowledged that she'd been hiding her concerns and could understand how frustrated Dr. Rick had become. However, she also knew that his tone and bluntness shut her down even more and that she needed to stand up to him. If she couldn't, she was aware that the research project was doomed: she'd continue to run from him. Because the stakes were high and Dr. Rick meant so much to her personally and professionally, Chloe wasn't prepared to just improvise on the spot the next time she dealt with his hot temper. She needed a script—the right words—so we aided her in constructing one that she could rehearse so she'd be prepared the next time she was caught off guard by Dr. Rick.

Rehearse, Rehearse, Rehearse

It's tough to catch your feelings in the moment. We know that if you have your words—your script—to run through ahead of time, you'll be less likely to use Displacement. Facing conflict and discomfort, accepting your right to stand up for yourself with those who threaten you the most, is a long and difficult battle for everyone. But with some language to lean on, you'll be less inclined to attack back or pounce on an innocent victim. Here's a five-step way to create your personal script.

Step 1

Remember the last scenario where you were caught with your "pants down."

- Did you want to run? Yell back? Cry?
- Did you smile politely and slink off?
- Did you freeze up and do nothing?
- How long afterward did you blast someone else?

Step 2

Continue to keep the scenario in your mind's eye, but this time see yourself with your feet firmly planted on the ground. Take three deep, slow breaths and stretch your fingers out to release tension.

Step 3

In your re-creation of the scenario, it's critical that you stave off the onslaught of words—and the feelings that arise from them and from within you. Put the brakes on by stating something like: "Please stop," "Wait a minute," or "Hold on a second."

Step 4

Next, it's essential to open your mouth and verbalize your emotions. Say:

- "I feel [sad, angry, ticked off, annoyed, hurt] when you . . ."

- "I shut down when you . . ."

- "I can't hear you when you . . ."

- "I get scared when you . . ."

Step 5

When the person you're struggling with doesn't let it go, berates you, or becomes more agitated, get away from the scene of the crime by stating:

- "I'm not comfortable."
- "I'm leaving now."
- "I'll talk to you later."

Of course you can't always know when you're going to be confronted by a situation that will trigger your Displacement, and it's impossible to rehearse for those unexpected times. But pay attention to those areas in your life that tend to worry or scare you the most, whether it's your job, your relationship with your significant other, or your family. Focus on how to improve the situation during a rehearsal and you'll be able to subtract that hand-me-down anger from your *real* world.

Still in the dark about Displacement? Take our quiz. Answer the questions honestly rather than just checking off what you're "supposed" to say.

Let's Say That . . .

1. Your wife starts an argument just as you're leaving for work, and now you're going to be late. Would you be more inclined to:

    a.   Tell her that you understand she's upset and you'll be home early to get together with her to talk it over.

    b.   Rush out with a knot in your gut, drive too fast, and honk loudly and curse at the driver who hesitates at a green light.

2. A houseguest breaks your washing machine and then leaves without offering to pay to fix it. Would you be more inclined to:

    a.   Call your friend once you have a repair estimate and offer to split the cost with her.

    b.   Rant and rave at the service technician over the price of fixing the machine.

3. Your son fumbles the ball and causes his team to lose the game. Would you be more inclined to:

a. Take your child aside and give him the "We can't win 'em all, and you did your best" speech.

b. Scream at the referee for being an idiot.

4. Your boss insists that you work through lunch, and you know that you'll go home ravenous and headachy. Would you be more inclined to:

a. Tell your boss that you'll be happy to do the job and suggest ordering in lunch for everyone.

b. Say nothing and then that evening make your tearful child sit at the table until her dinner plate is clean.

5. Your stylist cuts your hair way too short even though you gave her explicit instructions as to what you wanted. Would you be more inclined to:

a. Tell her that you're really not happy with the results and would like a discount.

b. Meet your sister at a restaurant and immediately berate her about buying those overpriced designer jeans—oh, and they make her butt look big!

If you answered more *b*'s than *a*'s . . . guess what? Displacement is your Defender of choice. And it may be time to start speaking up and stop paying your anger forward.

The Payoff

If we avoid an exchange that we perceive as threatening, we're likely to re-create it elsewhere just to *do* something with the pent-up feelings. But if we're brave enough to face the true source of our discomfort, we may find a great resolution and then move on with our lives.

Imagine how much more pleasant your life will be when you're no longer perceived as someone who can be relied upon to cause discomfort, pain, and fear with your misplaced harsh words and cruel behavior. Family, friends, and colleagues will no longer shrink from contact with you or avoid you altogether.

Better yet, envision how much more confident you'll feel about yourself when you're able to express your feelings unambiguously, say no when you feel uneasy or pressured, stand up for yourself without caving, and walk away from untenable situations with your head held high. You'll then be able to turn to others in your world for support and comfort, rather than using them as the scapegoat for your anger.

Chapter Seven

Listen to the Whole Story: Suspend *Sublimation*

Defendapedia

Sub·li·ma·tion (*suhb-luh-MEY-shuhn*): Channeling thoughts or feelings that are intolerable to you and/or to society at large into behaviors that are unobjectionable.

Krav Maga is an Israeli martial art that was brought over to the U.S. in the 1980s. Since then, this self-defense style has been adopted by those who protect and serve, including police departments and FBI and DEA agents. The philosophy behind Krav Maga was born of the need to teach people how to fight under the worst conditions when they're feeling the most disadvantaged. Like Krav Maga, this next Defender of the Heart, *Sublimation*, gives people a sense of empowerment—rather than feelings of defeat—in intolerable situations.

We are intimately aware of Krav Maga because we have friends and family members who are instructors. Although *we* aren't walking specimens of what this martial art does to a body, we do know some of the buff and talented men and women who practice and teach it. It has also become a useful tool for Hollywood stars, who call upon it when they need to get in shape or realistically perform many of their own stunts.

One gorgeous, great guy of our acquaintance springs to mind when talking about Krav Maga in connection with Sublimation.

Byron would walk down the street; and women, sometimes men, would get whiplash. He was "cut"; stood 6'2"; and had *café au lait* skin and an attractive, dimpled face. He came from one of the toughest neighborhoods of Los Angeles, and his family history sounded like something right off a police blotter. His father had left the house when Byron was four, leaving his mom working two jobs to support her four kids. When Byron was just 11, his 15-year-old brother, James, was killed in a drive-by shooting. His sister, Jackie, two years older than Byron, was then shipped off to North Carolina to live with an aunt. His oldest brother, Samuel, Jr., at 16 had already been running with a gang for a couple of years. He had been incarcerated in juvenile hall twice, and nothing seemed to get through to him. Byron's mom was barely treading water, and she was so worried for all her children.

Byron became active in the local Boys Club and began to wrestle in high school. As he grew bigger and stronger, he became obsessed with being active and tough. Because of his powerful body and competitive spirit, he found his way out of a difficult home life and neighborhood. Byron got into college but decided not to go for college sports. Instead, he became interested in martial arts and began to explore all forms of self-defense. Along the way, he won tournaments and earned a lot of respect. But it wasn't until he found Krav Maga that he knew what he really wanted to do: live, breathe, and teach this self-defense technique. While teaching it at the police academy, Byron realized where his life would be heading in the future: to law enforcement!

Everything that Byron had done up to this point had served to get him out of a debilitating situation so that he could make a better life for himself. On one level, this was a conscious commitment to do something unique. We believe that on a deeper level, Byron's obsessive passion and drive were a way for him to shift his excruciating internal feelings of deep grief and loss onto healthier and less dangerous ground.

We can only surmise that besides horrible sadness, Byron felt small and unprepared to fight the real and imagined wars happening around him. Somewhere deep within, he must have felt rage and wanted to retaliate against those who had harmed him and his family. But Byron was a good kid. His closeness to his mother and his sensitivity to her despair led him to make choices—some he was aware of, some not. He discovered a way to feed the roaring beast inside of him that was acceptable to him and society. Sublimation was primarily a positive method by which he dealt with his raw aggression and enormous, destructive fears. He rerouted his internal pain and found ways to come out the other side. He ultimately brought comfort, safety, and a constructive life to those around him.

Inspiration from Sublimation

If it weren't for Sublimation, all of us would be missing out every day on the positive contributions that are the end results of this Defender of the Heart.

Think about the pleasure you get from hearing music: soothing symphonies, contemporary love ballads, or even heavy metal. Do you rush home to watch Emeril Lagasse or Rachael Ray stir, mold, and bake their luscious goodies on the Food Network, and get turned on by the idea of making or tasting a decadent dessert? Do you ever feel emotions well up in you when looking at a photograph or a painting or while watching a movie that tickles your funny bone or tears at your heart?

Well, you can bet that many of these creative and delicious works of art blossomed out of Sublimation. From Pablo Picasso to Andy Warhol to the guy in sculpting class at the local community college or the child working on a finger-painting masterpiece . . . from Wolfgang Puck to Martha Stewart to the young woman in her own kitchen whipping up her first veal parmigiana . . . from Beethoven to Garth Brooks to the Seattle garage band to the kids in middle school orchestra . . . from Shakespeare to Arthur Miller to the incipient screenwriter revising his script to the boy working on his high school newspaper —it's quite likely *all* employed Sublimation.

Of course, we can't possibly have a clue about what goes on in the inner lives of all those famous and not-so-famous creative people, because we don't personally know them. What we *do* know for sure is that from early childhood, every one of us harbors deep feelings and conflicts. We choose certain paths for ourselves over time that satisfy and quiet these unconscious struggles.

Some turn out to be much more successful and rewarding than others. It's believed by many a theorist that this Defender of the Heart—this way of diverting internal distress and instinctive drives such as sex, aggression, and hunger that we all have inside—is the basis for inspiration and inventiveness.

Everywhere you look you can see evidence of what happens when human beings redirect their desires and impulses into satisfying and commendable deeds. But with every Defender of the Heart—even the much more mature and constructive examples like this one—there is always a downside. The negative part is that it can block you from being in a place where you can see more of the "whole picture": *your* whole picture. Every Defender steps in to divert some type of pain, uneasiness, and conflict you're oblivious to within yourself, even when the outcome is ultimately valuable.

Thank goodness that Bob—secretly irate that his neighbor's hanging bushes dripped crud onto his lawn—has his weekend biking club so that he can pedal away his fury, or else there would be hell to pay. If it weren't for Tom's intense workload, he might be in touch with the deep lust he feels toward the new receptionist. The bike club and the long hours at work are useful and effective measures for these guys. These activities help alleviate their unconscious struggles.

Although Bob knows that he's mad at this neighbor, he isn't aware of the murderous rages that stem from feeling used and abused. Tom knows he's turned on by the receptionist but can't face his sexual longing. The ways in which these two sublimate are working to protect them. And that's good. But as healthy as Sublimation is—no one wants the neighbor to be bludgeoned to death or the secretary to be taken on the desk!—it still hinders Bob and Tom from really feeling and growing from these distasteful, uncomfortable, socially unacceptable feelings.

What Bob doesn't let into his awareness is the possibility that he could deal with his fury in other ways as well. Maybe if he could withstand his anger and tolerate the discomfort it brings, he might get to know and even like this neighbor. Tom gets a lot done, and the company thrives because that's where he's planted his lustful impulses. Why not explore those desires more completely, acknowledge them, and quit working 100 hours a week? Tom could stop running from those urges and use them to spice up his ten-year marriage: after all, he works so much that his wife hasn't seen him for months!

Heart Beat

A recent study by researchers at Massachusetts General Hospital's Center for Mental Health and Media found that many children play violent video games to manage their feelings, including anger and stress. Bear in mind, though, that even socially acceptable forms of Sublimation such as these can still be psychologically unhealthy. For instance, other studies have shown that exposure to violent video games can desensitize people to real-life violence. And when the violence reaps some kind of reward on screen, it tends to increase hostility, as well as aggressive thinking and behavior in players. Violent acts that are punished in the game also increase hostility, but affect aggressive thoughts and behavior less. So make sure your chosen method of Sublimation isn't doing you more harm than good!

Ms. 101 Percent

Charlotte was a 59-year-old high-powered real-estate broker whom we first met a few years ago. She had begun a lucrative career in her late 20s after having two babies, and she'd never looked back. By the time California became the place where a postage-stamp-sized home was listed at more than $1 million, Charlotte was overseeing five agents and had a reputation for fairness and great business acumen.

Then, after she'd been hustling for a long time and had made a good name for herself, the housing market plummeted. Much to Charlotte's surprise—and to that of friends and family members who knew her well—she freaked out. She stopped eating properly, slept poorly, had trouble returning calls, and barely made it in to the office. Her worried husband begged her to seek some help, and that's how she got hooked up with us.

We'd heard of Charlotte and knew many people who had done business with her. Although we hadn't met her prior to our first appointment, we were stunned by the difference between the woman whose reputation had preceded her and the one who actually walked into our office. In front of us sat a deflated, scraggly haired person filled with self-doubt. We marveled that she had been unable to hold on to all the successes of the past and had instead been defeated by this temporary downslide in the market.

Immediately our minds went to the question: *what role had her work played all these years?* What got stirred up that made her run toward such feelings of failure? Why was she unable to put this tough bump in the road into perspective? After making sure that she was medically checked out and her sleeping and eating habits had gotten back on track, we delved into her history.

Charlotte came from a close, supportive family of high achievers. Her father was in the furniture business; her mother was a world-renowned architect; and her brother had followed in Mom's footsteps, teaching architecture and writing books on the subject. No one had ever made Charlotte feel "less than." Her parents and brother were always the first to support her, and they showed up no matter what she was pursuing. While her brother's artwork was hanging in gallery shows around town, the whole family was also in the front row applauding as Charlotte belted out "I'm Gonna Wash That Man Right Outa My Hair" in a high school production of *South Pacific*.

Everything that Charlotte touched turned to gold. She gave it all 101 percent. Surprisingly, she'd chosen to get married in her early 20s, becoming the best wife she knew how to be. Her parents hadn't been upset by her decision, but they *had* thought it was too early for her to settle down. Her mom had hoped that Charlotte would find something she loved to do professionally, just as *she* had done so many years before.

Over a period of time in therapy, Charlotte came to realize that she had chosen a healthy and successful way to divert unexplored feelings that had lain dormant inside her for decades. She was shocked when she gained insight into how she'd kept early "baby" wishes and resentments inside without having any clue that those feelings had colored her choices in life. She uncovered her envy toward her brother and her wish to be like him. In her mind, Charlotte had perceived him as sharing an intimate connection with their mother that she did not. This had left her feeling isolated, panic-stricken, and angry. She'd had to channel her private, unacceptable feelings elsewhere so that no harm would come to the people she needed and loved the most. To get away from those internal feelings, she had sublimated them all those years into being Ms. 101 Percent. None of this had been a product of conscious thought.

As is typical with those using this Defender, Charlotte instinctively guided her abhorrent feelings toward permissible behaviors, becoming the most successful, high-powered Realtor she could be. We assured her that inner drives, instincts, and unconscious thoughts are a part of all of our lives. There's nothing intrinsically wrong, bad, or destructive about such deeply held beliefs or feelings—they're normal. What we do with them makes up who we are; how we feel at the present time; and the choices we make in love, work, and play.

Charlotte took a good thing much too far. By sublimating those early intolerable feelings, she never revisited them, never knew she even *had* them. Her life plan became: *be successful, push through, avoid any possibility of failure.* When the real-estate market crashed, so did she. Failure was an unacceptable emotion to encounter—it was coming from without *and* within, and it was too much for her to allow.

In order to redirect those early feelings of despair, Charlotte channeled them into the pursuit of being the most successful person in her field, which she was for a long time. However, when she couldn't hold back the tide of oncoming catastrophe—the fall of the real-estate market on a grand scale—she, too, collapsed. She couldn't put this external failure into perspective, because never before had she been faced with anything like this. Because of outside circumstances, no longer could she be the best.

Sublimation takes what's unacceptable down into the basement of your mind and reconstitutes it into actions, activities, or behaviors that you, your family, and society can acceptably live with— and that's a good thing. But as you've gotten to know by now, too much of a good thing can be *not* such a good thing. Like all Defenders, Sublimation can get to a point where eventually it may turn against you by building walls around your heart. These barricades lock you in and limit you from knowing and understanding your deepest feelings. Being unaware of those feelings—the ones that are repugnant to you—and leaving them locked in your mind's basement leads you to live a life that's less than what you deserve.

Hot and Bothered

If you're at all familiar with the term *Sublimation,* we bet you think about it in the context of sex. When people take a cold shower after a hot date that wasn't consummated, they're cooling off their sexual feelings. They're literally and figuratively pushing down impulses that they aren't ready, or haven't been able, to act upon.

Think about the teenager who pounds the piano in the living room while her parents are in the kitchen with throbbing headaches. It's not hard to imagine that this kid is filled with raging hormones and angst, and music is her way of getting out her sexual tensions and aggressions. We all know that guy who absolutely has to brag about having the best, the biggest, the newest, and the most expensive toys. We ask ourselves, *What's he trying to prove? What size is his penis?* We're annoyed. We might laugh. But during quiet moments, we get it: it's all about feeling small and overcompensating. That's Sublimation at its sexual finest!

For others of you, when you hear the word *Sublimation,* those huge, hulking, in-great-shape men and women of the sports world come to mind. Here it takes the form of kicking the crap out of your opponent: channeling *aggressive* impulses into suitable actions. It's about slipping on your silky boxing shorts and lacing up your leather gloves, sweating as you furiously yet cautiously make contact with your adversary. It's about balls: funneling all that tension into smashing a little white one, heaving a brown pigskin across the field, dunking a big orange one into a net.

Oh, goodness . . . this sounds like sex again! And there truly is a marriage between aggressive feelings and sexuality. Both are expressions of primal urges. Sublimation is the matchmaker that places these human urges into "all right" situations for the individual and society.

It's a tough task to uncover those impulses and drives that are hidden from you in your unconscious. That's the craziest thing of all—to pay attention to something that your mind has asked you to *never* pay attention to. However, some feelings and reactions are more easily understood than others. By reviewing, suspending, and critiquing what you're doing in work, play, and love, you'll be exposing yourself to impulses that have been hidden for a long time. We're going to help you bring some of your actions and their meanings forward.

What's _Your_ Line?

There was a popular game show in the 1950s and '60s called _What's My Line?_ A panel of celebrities would be blindfolded, and out would come a "mystery guest," a person who had done something to garner attention—good, bad, or wacky. The audience would know what the guest's "line" was, but it was a mystery to the panel. Each celeb in turn would ask a question about the person. If it received a nod, the panel member would get the chance to dig deeper with another question, and so on, until he or she got to the bottom of the mystery.

In _our_ version of the game, you're the guest and we're the panel. We want you to start with what you know. We're going to help you figure out _if_ you're sublimating and _how_ it has served you up to this point.

If you answer yes to a question, dig deeper and ask yourself some follow-up queries. We've given you a few to start with. You will likely come up with some of your own as you recognize parts of yourself.

The questions have to resonate with feelings that you might have sublimated: you've been angry at someone; you're upset by the loss of something; you're disappointed about how things are going in your relationships with your partner, kids, family, and/or co-workers; you've been feeling ugly and undervalued for your femaleness or maleness; or you've been aching to be close to someone physically and emotionally. We can't know the exact reason why you might sublimate, but this is a way for you to ponder what the heck you're running from.

Remember that the purpose of exploring your Defenders is to get a better handle on them. With more awareness of how you tick, you have greater access to who you are, as well as to the clarity that will help you make the most gratifying choices for yourself.

Q: Are you first to arrive at work in the morning and last to leave at night? If yes, is it because . . .

. . . you just love your job so much?

. . . you'd rather be at work than at home?

. . . you get kudos from your co-workers?

. . . you think the firm expects it of their employees?

. . . you're someone who has always given 101 percent?

. . . you're afraid of losing your job?

Q: Are you at the gym every day, in addition to being the most competitive person in weekend pickup games? If yes, is it because . . .

. . . you're just a natural athlete?

. . . you're unhappy with the way you look and want to get in shape?

. . . it keeps you off the streets where you could get in trouble?

. . . if you didn't blow off steam in this way, you'd probably blow your top?

. . . it's an excuse to get out of the house?

Q: Do you get out your chain saw and trim the trees in your yard when the in-laws come to stay? If yes, do you do it because . . .

. . . those trees are way overdue for some maintenance?

. . . you want your in-laws to know what a good spouse you are?

. . . you hope to give your partner some alone time with his parents?

. . . you think the in-laws don't like you and you want to stay out of their way?

. . . you don't like *them* and you're afraid you'll go psycho on them?

Q: Are you constantly decorating and redecorating your home? If yes, do you do it because . . .

. . . you get bored easily and like change?

. . . once your house is "just right," you'll start having people over?

. . . you've been feeling disappointed by others recently?

. . . your sister's home always looks better than yours no matter what you do?

. . . the job you *really* covet is unavailable to you at this time?

Q: Are you drawn to a career in law enforcement or the military? If yes, is it because . . .

. . . you want to be one of the good guys?

. . . you like the power behind wearing a uniform and carrying a weapon?

. . . it's a legal way to kick some ass?

. . . you want to get the respect the uniform carries?

. . . it's a way to demonstrate your manliness or show that you're not a weak female?

Q: Do you burn hours playing online games, shopping on eBay, updating your page on a social-network Website, or staring at Internet porn? If yes, is it because . . .

. . . your everyday life is *so* boring?

. . . you have no real friends to hang out with?

. . . it gives you the opportunity to do things you can't do in real life?

. . . your online buddies seem to like you better than the people you know in person?

. . . you find your Internet pals more interesting than your family and friends?

Q: Are you a maniac on the dance floor? If yes, is it because . . .

. . . your fiancé is saving himself for marriage and this is the only way you get physical together?

. . . you don't have a partner and this is the next best thing to sex?

. . . you fantasize that you're dancing with your married neighbor whose bones you'd like to jump?

. . . you can "disappear" in the crowd and noise of the dance club?

. . . you're a really good dancer and love the attention you get?

Q: Are you childless, and do you dress your pet like a kid? If yes, do you do it because . . .

. . . you're just an animal lover?

. . . you'd be lonely without Fluffy or Fido to talk to?

. . . you like having something smaller than you to boss around?

. . . the loss of your last lover was too painful to bear, so now you only want the unconditional love of an animal?

. . . your pet doesn't talk back?

Q: Is your social life so busy that you haven't seen your family in ten years? If yes, is it because . . .

. . . you like your friends better?

. . . you want to show your family that you don't need them?

. . . you can never please them anyway?

. . . they make too many demands on you?

. . . their rejection of your spouse/profession/lifestyle is hurtful?

We're sure that you recognize yourself, or parts of yourself, in many of the preceding situations. Up to this point, some of your activities have kept you at a distance from your anger, fears, sadness, loneliness, lusts, and frustrations. Some of the ways you use Sublimation are more easily understood than other, subtler ones. It's pretty clear what you're sublimating if you get the chain saw out when your annoying in-laws show their faces at your door. Similarly, if—like Byron—you're someone who works in law enforcement, that's a commendable thing, but it's a career decision that may have roots in sublimated aggressions that have been redirected.

It might be less clear to you how some of the other "lines" are connected to the art of Sublimation. For instance, having a loving relationship with your pet is soothing. Studies show that blood pressure and overall health are positively affected by this connection. However, people who are childless may pour all their unexpressed love into their animals, using Sublimation as the coping mechanism to survive their losses.

Being more aware of the sadness around a loss doesn't change the reality that there is one. And Sublimation, as we've said, is a more mature and healthier Defender than most. But even in a pet-lady scenario, it might make her more well-rounded if she understood what her animals represented. It could allow her to use the time she'd taken in dressing her cat to instead reach out and address her need for others.

Did the question about being distant from your family resonate with you? Has it been forever since you spent quality time with your close relatives, yet you're a social butterfly with your peers? There are a lot of reasons why you might break off intimate ties with loved ones. It could hinge on your out-of-touch feelings of anger or resentment toward them. Possibly, down deep, you believe that you're a failure who hasn't lived up to their expectations and all you feel they demanded of you . . . so you've used Sublimation to cope.

The Payoff

Sublimation can be useful and can motivate you to achieve many things. But often it turns you into a plow horse with blinders on: plodding along, only glimpsing part of the glorious world around you. You deserve to see the whole picture—to understand the forces that make you "go"—and that means finding ways to acknowledge and ultimately accept what you carry inside. Although it can be helpful to distract yourself from intolerable ideas, undoubtedly you're better off developing a deeper understanding of yourself, your motivations, and your desires. Take time to be curious about why you chose to do what you do, and through this self-reflection, you can grow and become more satisfied with your life.

Chapter Eight

Stomach Your Angst Now: Put Off *Procrastination*

Defendapedia

Pro·cras·ti·na·tion (*proh-kras-tuh-NEY-shuhn*): Delaying tasks or actions that need to be started or completed as a way of steering clear of your uncomfortable, distressing internal angst.

On this beautiful, crisp Saturday morning, we've already consumed several cups of herbal tea, visited the bathroom down the hall countless times, ripped open the crackers and cheese in our office kitchen, and called our respective kids on a dozen occasions between us. Unfortunately, we enjoy each other's company and stories so much that we can chat about any and all things.

In other words, we've used any reason we can to put off delving into this new chapter: anticipating the anxiety of the day's writing ahead of us, having to think about it, getting stuck, becoming stirred up. Although we have a template of where we're headed when we start out, each chapter tends to ebb and flow and change direction as we push on toward the finish line. This interplay keeps us fresh and excited but also plays into our *Where are we going next?* and *Are we on the right track?* anxieties. This morning we're the victims of our own *Procrastination.* This Defender of the Heart that we so easily succumb to is protecting us from inevitable feelings of discomfort.

You can probably identify with us. Maybe you know that you need to start something, or perhaps you feel you want to finish something. A time frame has been set, whether by you or by someone else—just as we have a deadline for this book—but you just can't stick to it.

Everybody puts off the inevitable at some time or another. Think about when you've used this old delaying tactic. Was it during your school days: the completion of an academic exercise, finishing a research paper, or memorizing all the states in the Union? Is it in the workplace now: handing in the company budget, starting on the employee reviews, or updating the client files? Does it come about in a love relationship: keeping in contact with your sister, having that heart-to-heart with your elderly parent, or apologizing to your spouse after a big brouhaha? When you want to do something to better yourself—such as dieting and exercising, or stopping smoking cigarettes or pot—and the task feels too daunting, does Procrastination creep in?

Interestingly enough, the reason we're having a tough time facing the empty page is one of the primary reasons any of us procrastinates: perfectionism. Do you ever feel like you're supposed to know something right off the bat or accomplish a task with very little struggle or sweat? And if it doesn't flow easily from your brain, pen, or mouth, then it doesn't come at all? You tell yourself that if you have to grapple with something—if it doesn't progress naturally and it's not just wonderful the first time—then just forget the whole thing. You're most likely fighting a voice that's shouting in your head: *It's all or nothing!* You're in the throes of perfectionism.

This irksome way of being has some value. It propels you toward being the best you can be. But it's really a very painful double-edged sword. Those of you navigating with perfectionism as your copilot are never satisfied because your mind believes that you must be superhuman—but you'll always fall short. And then perfectionism's big sister, Procrastination, jumps in to stop you from making an ass of your human self. She puts the brakes on you, makes excuses for you, and facilitates your continuing under the misconception that you need to do everything right—just not right *now*.

You think this big sister is a godsend. You grab Procrastination's hand and believe that she'll protect you from your anxious state. The funny thing about this Defender is that it doesn't really protect you; instead, it grows a secondary uneasiness and doubt. The idea starts to bubble up in your brain that you don't have the goods to get things done, and an *I am a loser and a fake* mentality emerges. There's a bee in your bonnet that continually buzzes until the task is under way. It clearly triggers an ache not associated with the original discomfort.

So based on not doing what you intended to do, when you intended to do it, you're now immersed in feeling rotten about yourself. There is an urgency that starts to surface and leaves you with a new anxiety. With the onslaught of Procrastination comes the fallout: lack of confidence and growing disbelief in your abilities to get the job done.

And so you hide. You become more isolated and worry that someone is going to catch on to you and see that you're a fraud. In our practice, we constantly run across this feeling of *Someone is going to find me out; I'm just faking my way through.*

How can you ever feel successful if your favorite Defender is Procrastination? This question brings us to our favorite procrastinator.

Not-Lazy Lenny

We had a love/hate relationship with Lenny. At times we wanted to yell at him, and on other occasions we wanted to take him to the barber, so to speak, and sit back proudly as he got his first haircut. Although he was a successful general contractor, he was emotionally bound to his adolescence. Lenny had put his life, his adult competency, on hold. He'd been divorced for four years and had only recently bought a rug for his barren apartment. He was the father of two teenage girls and had always been close to them. Although they no longer wanted to hang with Dad, Lenny was caught up in wanting to know the latest on the girls' escapades. It was hard for him to acknowledge his 50-year-old self.

It had taken Lenny and his then-wife more than a year to finally get themselves into our office for couples therapy. They set the record for scheduling, canceling, and rescheduling appointments. Lenny's wife complained constantly that he was off in his own world, he didn't take any responsibility for the household, and she was tired of raising three kids: two daughters and a middle-aged "son."

It was clear that Lenny zoned out when it came to chores, helping the girls with homework, and following through on tasks he'd promised to complete. His wife was always furious at him for his extreme preoccupation with himself and his business, but she was also envious of his loving and close relationship with his daughters. After many years of fighting and feuding, and as the girls grew into young womanhood, Lenny and his wife chose to amicably divorce.

Over time, Lenny became one of the most involved and interested guys ever to walk through our office doors. After the divorce, he continued with his individual therapy. He zeroed in on his need to re-create the adolescence he felt had been denied him: his father had left when Lenny was ten, and he became his mother's partner in running the household.

From a kid who had been a good son, who had always been available and done things exactly to his mother's specifications, to the adult male who crossed his emotional arms, stood fast, and neglected grown-up tasks, Lenny had slid easily into using his Defender, Procrastination. However, through his therapy, he made great leaps toward taking responsibility for his actions and becoming more capable of achieving the little things that used to elude him. He even began to get his hair cut on a regular basis!

After always doing what he was told, without being given the room to grow into competency through his own successes and failures, the grown-up Lenny had been left with an anxiety that engulfed him. He'd lived for years in constant fear that he couldn't do things on his own. He worried that he would be unsuccessful if he made any attempt and would be ashamed and embarrassed by his failures.

Above everything, Lenny had somehow come to believe that to try wasn't enough; to succeed perfectly each time was his only option. The idea of failure or doing something over and over was repugnant to him. To counterbalance this pressured way of thinking, as an adult he unknowingly dug in his heels and held fast to the idea that he'd "get around" to things in his own time: the perfect gateway to Procrastination. No place was this more apparent than in the way he tackled his work life.

Lenny had been in the business of building commercial real estate for more than 25 years. He'd taken over a great business from his mother's brother. Uncle Max had loved his nephew, and Lenny spent summers working for him and learning the business. Max had his own way of running things, but when Lenny took over, he never seemed to catch up and get the business to run as smoothly as it had when Max was in control.

Lenny always seemed to fall behind on bids, scheduling meetings, and filing paperwork with the city. He was uncomfortable letting anyone know when he felt overwhelmed, out of control, and not perfect. Sitting amidst his overflowing desk and file cabinet with the door securely closed to the outside world, he'd jump on the computer and obsess about his stock 50 times a day.

Despite the lack of a smoothly run ship, the business thrived on Lenny's honesty and personality. When push came to shove, he always got the work done. However, what he suffered due to his procrastinating was far worse than ever losing an account. Lenny ate and drank too much and slept too little. This all had to do with the constant anxiety that he was falling behind and just couldn't muster the energy to get his act together. He was also depressed.

In therapy, we pointed out to Lenny just how nervous and pessimistic he was in our office and that he appeared to have been this way for a long time. He was astounded when he finally came to grips with how all those years he'd really seen himself as ineffectual and "little-boyish." Although he had been a husband and a father and had run a large business, he'd felt incompetent to make "manly" decisions. He had always doubted his choices and actions. After all, he'd had a loving mother who had ruled his life—telling him what to do and when to do it—in order to keep their life together afloat. She'd be pained to see her son struggle, so she would step in to pick up the slack of everything he tried before he could fail. Because of her own anxiety, Lenny had been subjected to a mom who couldn't stand to let him suffer the natural consequences of growing up.

This left him believing that he couldn't do anything; therefore, he doubted his own abilities. He never trusted his own judgment and expertise. If he had to struggle with a decision or an undertaking—if he was convinced it wouldn't come out perfectly the first time—why even try?

And with that, what we call a *Procrastination Pile* was born. We gave Lenny an exercise to do, which you can try, too.

Proverbial Procrastination Pile

When trying to get yourself motivated to begin that chore you've been avoiding, it's necessary that you first begin the "ordeal" by setting specific parameters. Don't bite off more than you can chew: you'll choke to death.

Buy yourself a cheap egg timer or use the alarm on your watch or cell phone. At the same time every weekday (you get the weekend off), take the timer or alarm to work, to your room, to the bathroom . . . to wherever that proverbial Procrastination Pile is expanding. Set it for ten minutes. That's it—that's the rule. Pick some papers, mail, photos, CDs, clothes, dishes—whatever your pile consists of—and get to work. File, organize, throw away, clean, read . . . whatever. When the timer goes off, stop: you're done for the day. Don't continue. Put it down. *Stop.* You'll return to it the next day. If you keep working on it, you're defeating the purpose of this exercise. *Live* with this. Over time, you'll be surprised by how much gets done. Delay that gratification and you *will* be gratified.

Lenny was wary of the whole notion of the Procrastination Pile exercise. He hemmed and hawed—*procrastinated*—for weeks, arguing that this ten-minute-rule thing was nuts. "It's stupid to stop doing something that I need to finish once I finally get started. I'll just have trouble getting back to it again."

We asked Lenny to trust us, stop whining, and just follow the rules of his assignment. We hypothesized that he was seeing us as his mother and was fighting against her intrusiveness through his lack of faith in our prescription. He was ticked off at us, but then he laughed and said that he *did* often feel like he wanted to battle us about our ideas and opinions. But he finally begrudgingly embarked on our mission. We laid down the law: no continuing to clean and organize files in his office after ten minutes. Whatever job he chose to conquer each morning might be the same one he delved into the day before, or not. It didn't matter.

By the second week, Lenny was still resistant, and distrusting of this "silly" activity. We were patient. That paid off because by week three, Lenny came into our office beaming. "It really is less overwhelming," he said. "Just knowing I have to return to the scene of the crime the next day seems to help me stop beating the crap out of myself for not finishing—and I'm finishing despite my resistance. And guess what? A by-product of this is that I'm feeling less jumpy and agitated inside. Work isn't freaking me out. I'm looking forward to going."

By subjecting himself to this initially uncomfortable experience, Lenny came to understand that he could do anything he set his mind to if he allowed his expectations of himself to be realistic. He began to have a better sense of his capabilities, realizing that if things became difficult, he didn't have to shut out the world and its demands. Instead, he could honestly feel inside that life would be okay, that he could pick himself up and be his own advocate. Through this very simple exercise (which he continued to practice almost daily years later)—and through his safe, supportive, yet challenging relationship with us—he learned that *taking small bites out of big things will eventually lead to success*. He became more tolerant of himself and his human imperfections. Although at times Lenny still found himself up against the proverbial Procrastination Piles of life, he was able to turn them around and not let them get the better of him.

Nothing to Fear But Fear Itself

We can all relate to putting off cleaning up that pile of junk, doing the bills, or filing paperwork. And our exercise is a great tool to get that type of chore under your control. But we imagine that you're asking, "How do I finish something bigger than a pile to file or donating clothes that I needed to get to Goodwill three years ago? How do I complete that one thing hanging over my head that I just can't do in a timely manner—the one thing I should do or there will be severe consequences . . . the one thing that, if completed, would make my life stress free for a while? And why don't I do it if I know the end result of not paying attention to it will be catastrophic?" To us, that speaks to just how powerful the reasons you don't move on it must be for you.

The one thing that eludes and haunts you might be the taxes you haven't filed, and now the penalties you've incurred are becoming outrageous. Or it's the life-insurance premiums you've been putting off paying, and now your policy is about to be canceled. Or Procrastination blocks you from seeking the medical evaluations you need, so you're suffering the extreme consequences of rotten teeth or high blood pressure that could have been tackled before they got out of hand. Perhaps your one thing is home repairs you've failed to pay attention to—not because the money wasn't available—and now the plumbing is failing or the termites have done almost irreparable damage and you have to spend thousands of dollars more.

Where do all these "I'll get around to it later" dilemmas come from? They originate from a place of fear. Sure, the perfectionism that drives you toward Procrastination is fear based—being afraid of looking like a fraud or not all pulled together. But apart from the dread of falling short of perfection, there are other fears that cause you to balk at getting things done. Some of them include: being embarrassed; being rejected; the unknown; conflict; success; and the fear of all fears, failure. These are the compelling reasons, however faulty they may be in reality, that keep you from acting.

There is a powerful saying we psychotherapists have adopted that is really appropriate for this Defender of the Heart:

F-E-A-R is False Evidence Appearing Real. It's taking bits and pieces of information that may or may not be true and acting and living as if they're gospel.

Most likely you have fears that developed in childhood, and you believe them to be real even today. They originated from exposure to many diverse people in your world and to various situations—some benign, some traumatic. As you got older, you held fast to a number of these fears, and your mind "believed" them to be true with very little—if any—"reality testing" in the moment to verify them. Often these fears were built around circumstances that left you with assumptions and discomfort you *knew* must be irrevocable. However, much of what was felt to be true for one time and place in your early life is most likely not so now . . . but you continue to live your life based on these outmoded beliefs.

Without your even realizing it, all these fears became great motivators to keep you *un*motivated. Fear is to blame for being paralyzed, sitting on your duff and procrastinating. The only way to get a grip on the fear that keeps you from achieving the one thing (or the second or third thing) that you're putting off is to have a clearer grasp of what the heck you're really afraid of. Reading our patient Jenny's story might give you some insight into your own.

Jenny's F-E-A-R

Jenny was swimming in fears that no longer held true for her: a living example of someone in the grip of False Evidence Appearing Real. As a kid of 12, she had repeatedly spent her entire allowance on makeup. Like so many parents, her mom remarked offhandedly, "Money just flows through your fingers. You'll never learn the value of a dollar, will you?"

Jenny was now a grown woman struggling to achieve success. Even though her supervisor had given her advice on how to get promoted, she put off doing what she needed to do to scale the management ladder and reach the pinnacle of her profession. She procrastinated with the best of us. Her F-E-A-R was that she couldn't hold on to riches—that success would slip through her fingers, just like her allowance had done so many years ago.

Look at how a small, seemingly inconsequential statement resonated with Jenny. Her mom's intentions were certainly not malicious, and all parents do and say things they haven't a clue will stick with their kids. It's not our intention to point fingers at mothers and fathers, but rather just to articulate how all of us "pick up" things that affect us, hold on to them, rework them, and live by them into adulthood. Naïvely, we take in information, make it our own, develop fears and convictions about ourselves and our place in the world, and fail to challenge them later in life.

Facing Your Own Fears

Revealing the fear that keeps you trapped will help you lower this Defender. Start working *backward* to find out what's keeping you from being propelled *forward!*

Figure out what you fear will happen when you complete the task you've been putting off:

- Others will be envious of you.

- You'll be obliged to keep going and don't know if you can.

- You may be called out on it and have to defend yourself.

- It will separate you from the rest of the group: your friends, family, or community.

- You'll do it wrong and have to redo it.

- It won't live up to your own standards or be good enough for someone else.

- Finishing it will only lead you to have to do more work.

- You won't be able to control the outcome or how others may respond to you.

- You'll gain some information that upsets you.

- You'll make a fool of yourself and people will laugh at you.

- You might have to ruffle someone's feathers and you'd rather just keep the peace.

You probably connected with some of these reasons or have come up with a few of your own. Now that you have an idea about what you're afraid will take place when you tackle a task and finish it, pick the one or two examples that resonate with you most and write out in detail what it is that you fear happening. Don't hold back; just let your anxieties run riot. Remember that this is all about False Evidence Appearing Real. Then, after you've done that, rewrite the potential outcome as a realistic worst-case scenario. In all cases when you find you're going into Procrastination mode, make this your mantra:

Really, what's the worst that can happen?

To get you started, here are some examples of what we mean.

Fear of Envy

— **Fear-Based Imagined Scenario:** If I ever get around to applying for that promotion, the women at work will be rude and nasty behind my back. They'll claim that I lied and cheated to get it. No one (except for the people who are suck-ups) will want to hang out with me anymore, and I'll have to eat lunch by myself. My sister will pout and make me feel guilty because I'm doing better than she is. My mom has always been jealous that she didn't get to have a career like I do and won't even say a word about it.

— **Realistic Worst-Case Scenario:** When I apply for a promotion, my co-workers will probably ask me what took me so long. Since I've never lied or cheated, there will be plenty of people who can shoot *that* rumor down before it even gets started. Sure, there will always be a few rotten apples who will be green with envy, but why do I care what they think, anyway? Even if people become a bit intimidated by my new status, *I* can always invite *them* to lunch. My sister and I have always been rivals, but I won't rub it in her face, and we're close enough that we can talk—and maybe even joke—about it. If Mom doesn't come through with the kudos, I'll just throw *myself* a big party!

Fear of Embarrassment

— **Fear-Based Imagined Scenario:** I can't try out for the lead in the play before I take another course in acting because I'll just make a fool of myself. Everyone will fall down laughing. Knowing me, I'll just make things even worse by blurting out some totally lame excuse for doing so badly: "The dog ate my script" or "I have a sore throat." I'll go down in flames and will never be able to show my face at the community theater again. Everyone will think I'm a joke.

— **Realistic Worst-Case Scenario:** I've already taken acting lessons, and my teachers have been honest about my strengths and weaknesses. I think I can handle this part, but lots of other people will be trying out for it, too, and most of them are probably as nervous as I am. If I do flub the audition, I won't be the only one, and others will be more likely to "feel my pain" than laugh at me. If I don't get the lead, perhaps I'll land some other part or even just work behind the scenes. I've always enjoyed that in the past. And there's always next year.

Fear of Rejection

— **Fear-Based Imagined Scenario:** I know exactly what will happen if I finally get up the courage to ask that cute girl at the gym to go out with me. Yes, she's been smiling at me and always says hi, but it's probably because she feels sorry for me and my puny body. If I ask her for a date, she won't even be friendly with me anymore and will tell all her jock friends how I crossed the line. Then those guys won't talk to me and give me workout tips anymore. I'll have to stop going to the health club and will just sit home watching TV by myself, getting fatter and fatter.

— **Realistic Worst-Case Scenario:** I've been going to the gym now for six months, and everyone there is really friendly. The cute girl seems very approachable, and I have no reason to think that she'd shoot me down if I asked her out. Maybe she's even been hinting for me to do it. If I actually get around to it and she does say no, it might be because she's involved with somebody or for another reason that has nothing to do with me. At least I will have broken the ice with her, and perhaps we can become gym buddies.

Fear of the Unknown

— **Fear-Based Imagined Scenario:** Those unopened credit-card statements have been piling up on my desk, and they make me sick to my stomach every time I look at them. The accounts are probably reaching their credit limits and racking up interest and late-payment fees, but I don't know for sure just how much I owe. If I open them, I might find out that I'm so far in debt that I can't get out. I might even have to declare bankruptcy or sell my house. I'll probably have to live in a tent under a freeway overpass!

— **Realistic Worst-Case Scenario:** I'll open the statements and make an assessment of the true picture of my finances. Yes, I've run up a lot of debt, but hiding my head in the sand is just making things worse. It might not be as bad as I imagined, and I've been making myself sick over nothing. On the other hand, it might indeed be bad, but I can stop the situation from escalating by calling the banks and negotiating a lower interest rate and working out a payment schedule. I'll have to cut up my credit cards and tighten my belt until I'm out of trouble. There'll be no more $500 Jimmy Choo shoes for a while.

Fear of Failure

— **Fear-Based Imagined Scenario:** So after years of talking about it, I want to quit my job and go into business for myself. However, I'll turn out to be a terrible entrepreneur. Nobody will want the services I'm providing or the products I'm selling. I'll have to plunder my kids' college funds and get a second mortgage on my house to stay afloat. We'll lose everything. I won't get hired by another company because I've burned all my bridges. My wife will leave me and take the children with her. They'll never speak to me again, and I'll end up a sad old man on the unemployment line.

— **Realistic Worst-Case Scenario:** I'll do my homework and make a solid business plan to make sure my proposed endeavor is viable before I quit my job. I'll also make sure that my new venture is properly funded. I'll maintain good relationships with people in my former field of employment. Maybe I'll even work part-time until the new venture is up and running. If the business does go belly-up (and many new businesses do fail), I'll discuss all the options with my wife. We'll come up with a contingency plan to get back on our feet. Perhaps I'll have to sling burgers for a while.

Don't all those fear-based scenarios now sound a bit overwrought? It's easy to see how you use this conveniently *in*convenient way to distance yourself from what you want most in life—love, contact, help, and support—when you write them out in this way. But what now?

It's one thing to recognize how you're using Procrastination; it's another to get started managing it. By its very nature, this particular Defender of the Heart is a tough one to crack.

Here are some guidelines to get you started:

— **Visualize yourself doing the task,** taking the plunge, making the change. If you can't even *picture* yourself doing it, the chances of your *actually* doing it are pretty slim. This technique is used a lot by athletes and actors. They practice or rehearse in their heads. There's some scientific validity to this, because the brain uses the same neural pathways to imagine doing an activity as it does when you're actually performing it.

— **Follow our ten-minute rule.** You already know it worked for our friend Lenny. Doing things in small increments really helps.

— **Don't try to do everything at once;** you'll get overwhelmed. If you're a mass procrastinator, tackle either the easiest task or the hardest one first—whichever you think will motivate you the most. You might want to get the tough stuff out of the way first because it will all be a piece of cake after that. Or you could be someone who's more encouraged by starting out small and building up to the most challenging undertaking.

— **Make it fun.** Create an air of excitement around what you're doing. And remember that you don't have to do everything perfectly. Quite often the gratification is in the process rather than the end result.

— **Reward your efforts.** Treat yourself to a movie or a massage after completing something you've been putting off. Or just take some time to luxuriate in your new state of not having something hanging over your head that you really "ought" to be doing.

Heart Beat

In a study at The Ohio State University, students who were the worst procrastinators in a college course with a lot of deadlines received significantly lower grades than did those who were low procrastinators. The most severe procrastinators earned an average grade of 2.9 on a 4.0 scale, while low ones scored an average of 3.6. The worst procrastinators also made excuses such as "I work best under pressure" to justify their behavior. The results clearly show that, in fact, procrastinators *don't* work better under pressure. Further, they probably don't have any idea how well they might do if they didn't procrastinate. Their low grades only go to show that these excuses are nothing more than . . . well, *excuses*.

The Payoff

Putting life's responsibilities on the back burner keeps you in your own head, constantly mired in discomfort. But when you stop procrastinating, the consequences are amazing. You'll experience the ramifications on so many levels. You become available to grab at life's brass rings as they come along; you stand the chance of fulfilling your dreams; you feel great about yourself; and most important, you're open when it comes to establishing and maintaining healthy and dynamic relationships.

The dull ache, the drone, that has dwelt inside you and kept you from being present for yourself and others dissipates. Letting down this Defender of the Heart opens you up to opportunities in the work world and assists you in recognizing the value of the people already a part of your life. You'll go a long way toward ensuring that your life is not one full of regret for missed chances and longings for what might have been.

Chapter Nine

Take Care of Yourself: Ease Up on *Altruism*

Defendapedia

Al·tru·ism (*AL-troo-iz-uhm*): Giving of yourself—whether time, money, or energy—in a way that both gratifies and wards off your own desires and needs. The word derives from the French *autrui* (other people), which in turn comes from the Latin *alter* (other).

We needed to get out of our office for a little while before we got started on this chapter. Actually, we were chomping at the bit for a vacation, but a walk around our neighborhood mall was all we could take time for. It's December, so bear with our thoughts, even though it might be summer as *you* read this.

Despite the fact that the air is often crisp, sunny, and bright here in Los Angeles at this time of the year, it stills seems fraught with doom and gloom for many folks. The holiday season stirs up a lot of deep emotions.

Memories of joyous past family gatherings make you smile. Wistfully, you remember how long it's been since Aunt Betty was alive. Excitement over your baby's first Christmas sends you running to the store to spend more than you can afford this year. The food, the smells, the sounds, and being around all your siblings and cousins excites you. However, knowing that your mom is setting up for the big family dinner and you're still in an ugly fight with your brother George is worrisome and makes you sick to your stomach. For some of you, longing to be with the family you *wish* you had and struggling with the one you've got is more painful than the Visa statement to come in January.

The holidays are also a time when giving to others less fortunate becomes an annual ritual. As you walk in the mall, the Salvation Army volunteer rings a bell and reminds you that there are many ways to share your fortunes, however large or meager they might be. Acts of generosity are expected at holiday time. Undoubtedly, you're aware that those checks you write at the end of the year can be deducted when you file your taxes. We don't want to sound too cynical, but giving and getting back something in return are intrinsically linked. *Altruism,* one of the kindest and most acceptable Defenders of the Heart, is both the act of giving *and* getting.

On the subject of Christmas, no one epitomizes the spirit of Altruism more than Santa Claus. Here's a guy well past retirement age, yet every year after Thanksgiving, he drags himself out to malls everywhere to patiently sit and listen to the wants and wishes of all those sticky little kids. Come the big night, he goes out in the worst weather of the year and single-handedly attempts to make all those dreams come true. He's fueled entirely by homemade cookies, which give him a belly that must be hell to stuff down those sooty chimneys. And that's after a full year of list making, toy manufacturing, and reindeer husbandry.

You'd think by now he'd have the kids text-message him their lists, outsource the toys to China, and get UPS to deliver them so that he could spend Christmas Eve like the rest of us: with his feet up, drinking eggnog, and watching *It's a Wonderful Life*. But out of the goodness of his heart, he keeps the tradition going, bringing wonder and joy to millions of lives. You know from the twinkle in his eye and his ever-ready "Ho, ho, ho" that he's getting his jollies from doing it.

The purest form of this Defender is giving . . . and getting self-satisfaction just from knowing that others benefit from your good deeds. Aptly, as we were thinking about Altruism during the holidays, stories about sharing were hitting the airwaves and newspapers. One feature that got a lot of press concerned a wealthy Kansas City businessman who's a real-life "Secret Santa." He took over the role when a good friend, another wealthy businessman named Larry Stewart, passed away. Stewart had once been homeless and down on his luck, but he turned his life around and his fortunes increased. For 26 years he walked the streets and personally handed out more than $1 million.

New Santa, who wants to remain anonymous, talked about his friend with reverence. "He'd hand [someone] a hundred dollars. . . . All he would ask is that you do something nice for somebody, and pass the kindness on," he said in an interview on ABC. In his first year of walking in his friend's boots, New Santa's Altruism changed the luck of 600 strangers. He believes that if $100 can inspire 1,000 people to carry out a random act of kindness for someone else, it's an investment worth making.

Money is only one shape that Altruism assumes. Taking action to assist others facing their own personal hardships is another. Bringing "Meals On Wheels" to the sick or elderly, working on a soup-kitchen line, walking the dog for someone who is out of town, working as a camp counselor for kids with disabilities, reading to kindergartners at the local library, being a search-and-rescue volunteer, and a multitude of other ways to "do good" in the most positive sense are what makes this Defender so beloved. Everyone who performs hands-on acts of compassion gets a healthy dose of self-gratification from the deed. Your best intentions and actions are noble and honorable and feel selfless to you. In fact, they've originated from your deepest yearnings and desires to feel loved, safe, and less isolated and alone in the world.

Then there are those people who aren't merely part-time volunteers but have chosen to devote their lives to being of service to others. By virtue of the professions they chose, they are totally immersed in a giving of self. Have you read about the couple who moved to Africa to work with dying babies? How about Doctors Without Borders? Surely you've heard about the chaplain in the ER who comforts grieving families? Or the social worker whose beat is downtown's skid row, with its homeless mothers and children? Remember your favorite elementary-school teacher who put up with spitballs in her hair? How about community activists who work full-time getting the recreation centers open in under-developed areas? Or the person who runs a blood bank and drives to outlying areas too remote for anyone else to visit?

Thank heaven for these generous souls. Such expressions of Altruism help others survive, grow, and live better lives. At the same time, these people who put their lives on the line, constantly deplete their energy, or push their finances to the limit welcome the prospect of gaining comfort and internal peace from their selflessness.

Good Grief

Although it's difficult to grasp, sometimes Altruism is rooted in a false belief that everyone is more worthy than you. So you work overtime—not only for the conscious satisfaction of watching others benefit from your charity, but also because it's the only way you can believe you have any value at all. Sometimes Altruism emerges from believing in your core that you'll be abandoned if you aren't everything to everybody. And occasionally Altruism's beginnings are so deep-rooted that you have no awareness that some place within you is feeling, *If I do for you, how could you not do the same for me?* Doing good works is a most constructive way to add fulfillment to your life, while at the same time relieving some of your anxiety—just like all good Defenders!

It's worth repeating how important a Defender Altruism is to you and humanity. But like all habits and attitudes of its kind, Altruism has the possibility of being so entrenched that it does the opposite of what it was intended to do. Sigmund Freud's daughter Anna grew up to be an important voice in the psychology world. In 1936, she published her noteworthy book *The Ego and the Mechanisms of Defense.* She went beyond her papa's thinking when she discovered a new way of viewing Altruism, which she called *altruistic surrender.* This concept turned the healthy part of Altruism upside down and revealed how too much of a good thing prevents you from living life to its fullest potential. Anna knew that if living for others was your only way of existing, you were surely ignoring your own needs and special gifts. Anna was on to something . . . and she would have had a field day with our friend Norman!

Noble Norman

Down the hall from our office suite is a nonprofit agency. Whenever we bump into anyone who works there in the hallway, the elevator, or the coffee shop downstairs, the person is invariably outgoing and cheery. The main man who keeps the place humming is Norman, the office manager. Over the years, he has become a friend, and we share many a raunchy joke with him. Norman has a way about him that encourages others to share their secrets. He would have made a great and compassionate therapist. Although he's an expert at getting people to open up to him, it took us many years to really get to know *him.* And we're usually two *yentas* who unearth intimate details pretty quickly!

Norman has a fascinating past. For many years he lived overseas and worked as a post-op nurse with kids recovering from cleft-palate and facial-reconstructive surgeries. He spent years in developing-world countries, rarely making it home to the U.S. But that was okay, because he loved caring for the kids who came to live in the hospital for months at a time and their families. He became a family member to many and would even travel far into remote regions to check up on the progress of "his kids" when he had time off. Even though Norman was making very little money, he would spend a lot of his hard-earned pittance on bringing these families the necessities they couldn't afford themselves.

After nine years in the field, Norman was sent home by the organization he worked for. He told us that he'd been working so hard that the agency believed he wasn't taking good care of himself. Having come down with a parasite he couldn't shake, he'd been losing weight and his health was at risk. After he returned to the States, it took some months for his body to recover. Norman's mom passed away during his health-induced hiatus, and he felt obligated to care for his father. Rather than return to his past life, he recognized the need to make some good money and stay close to family.

Due to his skills in post-op care for reconstructive surgery, Norman was hired by a group of high-powered plastic surgeons who owned several surgery centers around Southern California. For 15 years he dealt with the antithesis of what he'd worked with overseas. Here, most of the people he comforted, bathed, changed dressings for, and dispensed medications to were electing to have work done on themselves. But that didn't stop Norman from giving 100 percent of himself.

Norman described to us his 24-hour on-call duties in private home nursing and "concierge" services. He painted a picture of how he'd been at the patients' beck and call. If dry cleaning needed to be picked up, Norman did it. If the dog needed a walk or a bath, Norman did it. If his patient needed to call her business manager to set up a meeting, Norman did that, too. He even got good at hair and makeup!

Norman couldn't say no and felt that it was his responsibility to do whatever it took to make someone else's life more bearable. There was always great affection and joy in the way he delivered these nursing and other assorted services. As he wittily and uncomplainingly recounted these sometimes painful scenarios to us, we wondered if he might have walked on water!

One day Norman took us to lunch. We were curious about how he'd gone from "super nurse" to office manager. With a subdued demeanor, uncharacteristic of his personality, he shared with us how he'd had a meltdown after 12 years on the job. He had his first panic attack at age 48, leaving him frightened and stunned. Over the next year, he had bouts of panic and insomnia that caused him to fall asleep on the job during the day. Through a trusted friend he found a psychiatrist who put him on medication and recommended that he take a leave of absence.

It took Norman another two years to realize that he was burned-out and had to leave his job. Although friends had told him to slow down, to stop being the patients' errand boy and just focus on the nursing, Norman didn't think he could do it any other way. Toward the end of his private-nursing career, he acknowledged that he had no patience left for his patients! He didn't like them anymore, he didn't want to care for them, and he hated their dogs! He was appalled at himself but recognized something was askew . . . and it was *him!*

Norman came to the office-manager position with the hope that this new job would have clear boundaries in place. After those grueling years of panic and sleep deprivation, he finally paid attention to the fact that he'd never set limits on himself and had allowed others around him to take advantage of his bighearted nature. Norman told us that he still had the tendency to work over and above the call of duty. He recognized that when he volunteered to run the fund-raiser or seemed to stay later and later at the office to fix a spreadsheet or "tidy up," he'd come home exhausted. He'd go to bed without dinner, without returning a phone call from a good friend, or forgetting to check in with his dad.

Norman was worried that some of his old patterns of being "indispensable" to others were creeping back, even at this office job. He joked that he'd really taken us to lunch for some free advice. With tongue planted loosely in his cheek, he wondered how he could put a halt to being such a "dipshit" and a sucker. He knew by now that he was terrific at what he did and was invaluable to the agency. So why was it so difficult to set his parameters, care for himself, and still continue to do helpful work without burnout?

Norman needed some kind of barometer to gauge when his Altruism turned into "altruistic surrender"— when he was in the process of doing beneficial acts for others at his own physical and psychological expense. He needed some sort of "thingamabob" to help assess the toll his generosity was taking on him. Unbeknownst to him, he had come up with the perfect lingo: his "dipshit" picture of himself was a great way to wrap our heads around this concept. We bantered back and forth with Norman and used his depiction of himself to come up with the following dipshit index, or "dipstick."

Don't Be a "Dipshit"—
Monitor Your Internal "Dipstick"

Take a cue from Norman and try this **S-T-I-C-K** exercise for yourself.

<u>S</u>crutinize

Take some time to really examine what you've done for others. In your notebook, make three headings—"Today," "The Last Week," and "The Last Month"—and under them, write down the following:

- Any volunteer work you did, whether it was sitting on the board of a nonprofit organization or participating in tree planting in your area

- All those little favors you did for friends

- The extra load you took on at work for no additional pay

- The family chores you automatically did yourself and didn't delegate to your spouse or kids

- The tasks you took on for your church, your kids' school, or the neighborhood organization

- The money you gave to a homeless person

- Your donation to a thrift shop

- The Girl Scout cookies or magazines sub-scriptions you bought from a kid but didn't really want

- The times you undercharged for a job because you thought the customer couldn't afford your rates

- All those occasions when you took the smallest piece of pie or the burned toast

- The time you gave all your change to someone for his or her parking meter and then didn't have any for your own

- Your participation in a blood drive

Take an Altruistic Inventory

Now examine your list and honestly consider these questions:

- Are you doing less than you expect of your-self? Is your list embarrassingly meager? Does looking at it make you feel self-absorbed and uncharitable?

- Are you doing more than you expect of your-self? Does your lengthy list make it clear that you're being a "patsy"? Are you spreading yourself too thin?

- Are you content with the amount you're doing? Is your life well balanced between taking care of yourself and doing for others? Does looking at your list give you satisfaction?

Investigate Yourself

It's time now to do a self-inventory. Write down the last time you did something like the following purely for the pleasure of it and your own self-gratification:

- Took a long lunch
- Called a friend to go for a walk
- Had a brandy and a cigar
- Got a manicure or a massage
- Took a long weekend away from the kids
- Read a trashy novel
- Shot some baskets at the park
- Just sat and listened to music
- Went dancing
- Ate a cupcake
- Visited a museum
- Took a class in a subject that interested you
- Bought yourself flowers

Consider the Evidence

Now examine your list and honestly consider these questions:

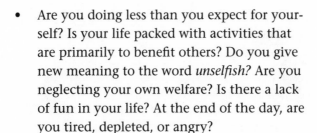
- Are you doing less than you expect for your-self? Is your life packed with activities that are primarily to benefit others? Do you give new meaning to the word *unselfish?* Are you neglecting your own welfare? Is there a lack of fun in your life? At the end of the day, are you tired, depleted, or angry?

- Are you doing more than you expect for yourself? Is your life all about "me, me, me"? Are your activities weighted on the side of self-gratification? Do you think everyone should be able to take care of themselves?

- Are you content with the amount you're doing for yourself? After you've done what you could for others, do you still have enough energy left to do something pleasur-able for yourself? Are you able to enjoy your leisure time guilt free because you've given what you can?

<u>K</u>eep It in Perspective

It's not selfish to care for yourself—it opens space to care for others. When flight attendants on a plane give the "safety talk," they always tell you that should it become necessary, you must put the oxygen mask on yourself before attending to those around you. This is because you can't help anyone else if *you* can't breathe! The same applies in life. Take a breath and adopt an Altruistic approach to your *own* life first. Nurture:

- Your **body** with good nutrition, physical activity, play, relaxation exercises, and plenty of sleep

- Your **mind** by telling yourself that you're every bit as worthy of your time and care as everyone else. Persuade yourself that you don't need to be a doormat to be useful

- Your **emotions** by looking out for yourself in the context of your relationships at home and at work

- Your **spirit** by honoring your creativity, sexuality, and beliefs

Then, when you're energized and relaxed, continue to do good works for others. Figure out how to give of your time, money, empathy, and energy without depleting yourself.

Once Norman had done this exercise, he began to realize in retrospect that his burnout from Altruism had left him with a hole in his heart. He really missed being a nurse. It was also a huge loss for his potential patients and their families because of how talented he had been in that field.

Heart Beat

A large nationwide survey on Altruism and empathy conducted by the National Opinion Research Center at the University of Chicago found that those who have strong feelings of love for people in general are more likely to have strong romantic relationships. The survey takers who scored high on questions about Altruism were more likely to rate their marriages in particular and their lives in general as "very happy."

Additionally, married people were more likely to rank high on altruistic love than those who weren't married. Forty percent of married individuals scored in the top category on Altruism, but only 20 percent of those who had never been married and 26 to 28 percent of the divorced or separated participants had top scores in that area.

If you're still not sure that your Altruism has crossed the line, read this:

You May Be Too Good for Your Own Good If . . .

. . . you always give yourself the overcooked end of the meat, the broken cookie, and the underripe fruit, but you never take the last chocolate, the biggest slice of pie, or the crunchy top of the mac and cheese.

. . . you donate money to anyone who asks for it—even if you can't really afford it—because you don't want others to think that you're mean.

. . . you're the one whom the PTA always calls on to volunteer for events on weekends or holidays.

. . . you're constantly at your family's beck and call and change your own plans to suit theirs.

. . . you spend your time at a party helping the host or hostess serve the food and clean up instead of socializing and having a good time.

. . . you don't take a well-paying job you'd love to have because it seems "frivolous" and you should be doing something more "worthy."

. . . you only buy something nice for yourself if you're also able to bring home something for the kids.

. . . you don't pursue a hobby or pastime you enjoy, as it has no social value.

. . . you resent other people who seem to kick up their heels and have a good time purely for the sake of it.

The Payoff

As with Humor, this Defender of the Heart results from too much of a good thing. When you take extra-good care of everyone around you, you may end up depleted. That, ironically, will limit your ability to help both others and yourself. You don't have the time or energy to commit yourself more deeply professionally or personally.

But when you're able to get a handle on Altruism, it can enrich your life considerably. When this Defender is lowered to an appropriate level, you'll end up feeling satisfied and filled with pleasure, not angry or resentful. As a bonus, when you're generous of spirit and deed and aware of your own boundaries, you're less likely to grapple with depression.

Chapter Ten

Cultivate Consciousness:
Alleviate *Passive-Aggression*

Defendapedia

Pas·sive-Ag·gres·sion (*PAS-iv-uh-GRESH-uhn*): Unassertively and indirectly expressing feelings of resentment, hostility, or hurt toward others.

You know by now that we live in Los Angeles. Our lives, families, and psychotherapy practices are smackdab in the middle of this sprawling city—one that reminds us of an animal with a multitude of tentacles running from its center.

These tentacles are our freeways. Many people spend long, tedious periods of time on them, commuting hours to and from work every weekday, with no escape even when they go out to play on weekends. It's no wonder we L.A. residents are obsessed with our vehicles. A study has shown that most people keep their cars for nine and a half years, but don't tell *us* that!

Not only do we want the newest, hippest vehicle on the market, we also desire the fanciest, most up-to-date gadgets. Bells and whistles abound; and we're pretty sure that by the year 2020, your car will cook you a pasta dinner while you wait at a traffic light. In the meantime, though, directional technology is the accoutrement *du jour.* To feel safer, less lonely, and more capable of navigating this treacherous tentacled beast, many Los Angelenos equip their cars with GPS (Global Positioning System) devices.

However, no matter what fancy-schmancy apparatus you own to help you move through the maze, these systems aren't foolproof. Often the directions they give are incorrect, or infuriatingly guide you along a circuitous route that takes longer than it should to reach your destination. Surprisingly, it becomes evident that you've relinquished your own capabilities and instincts to this machine. You take a backseat to the gadget until you start to realize that your journey is taking too long and *Where the heck am I?* begins to creep into your consciousness. You've allowed something else to think for you, so you're no longer an active participant in your own voyage.

Just like these navigational devices, our final Defender of the Heart, *Passive-Aggression,* can appear to be a comfort in times of chaos. At first glance, both the navigational device and the Defender are helpful because they distance you from your distress in the moment. The GPS device dials down your anxiety when you're trying to navigate the complex streets of a city. Passive-Aggression takes you away from the complex feelings of anger that you can't imagine facing head-on.

Both methods let you off the hook so that you don't have to be in complete control and personally responsible for any outcome that might occur. The difference is that although the navigational system will get you where you want to be in the long run, your Passive-Aggression Defender will *not*.

Sidestepping

Passive-Aggression is one of those Defenders that are now a part of our everyday lexicon. Think about the number of times you've heard someone being described like this: "He's so passive-aggressive," or "She's just such a passive-aggressive person!" You yourself might have used that label in speaking about other people. Why? What have they done to you or someone else to elicit that unattractive description? Most likely you've blurted it out because you've experienced this type of behavior from them (or others) before, and you just can't stand it any longer.

For example:

— You have dinner plans with a friend whom you recently had an argument with. An hour before you're supposed to meet at the restaurant, she leaves a voice message saying that she just can't make it tonight. This isn't the first time she's left you hanging after you've had a disagreement.

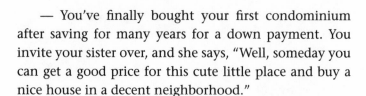

— You've finally bought your first condominium after saving for many years for a down payment. You invite your sister over, and she says, "Well, someday you can get a good price for this cute little place and buy a nice house in a decent neighborhood."

— How about the anonymous nasty letter you receive from someone in the neighborhood about not picking up after your dog? You're left holding the bag (pun intended) and can't respond directly to this unfair, oblique attack.

— Your mother-in-law comes to dinner, and she "kindly" aligns herself with you, commenting that it's no wonder it's too tough to keep your house in order when you work so hard.

— Your husband promises to be home by 6:30 every evening yet consistently comes in around 8 or 9. When you ask him to please try to be home for a special dinner, he says, "Of course," but once again flies in at 8 P.M. spouting all kinds of flimsy excuses.

These actions and responses are clear examples of this Passive-Aggression Defender. All these people are acting out spiteful feelings they may or may not be aware of having. Wherever their hostility stems from—be it envy, fear of being left out, or worry about getting too close or relying on someone else—passive-aggressive types can't, or are unwilling to, uncover those difficult feelings within themselves. They're unable to speak their emotional truths directly and kindly. This leaves those who rely on this Defender with an icky sensation of disgust, remorse, self-doubt, and self-loathing. In turn, they feel alone and disconnected and are almost always left with a kernel of uncertainty about how much they're really loved.

At one time or another, we all struggle with being aware of the emotional truths that resonate inside of us. Being direct and calmly confrontational with others when you feel threatened or disappointed or your expectations of them have been shattered isn't an easy road for anyone. But if you're less experienced at dealing with your feelings up front and are worried about the consequences of your anger, you might have a tougher time being cognizant of those feelings. Passive-Aggression then becomes less a "once in a while" mistake and more a way of being.

It's easier to spot this Defender in others than to recognize it in yourself. (But don't get too comfortable; *your* time on the Passive-Aggression hot seat is coming up!) It starts out with the passive-aggressive person dropping "smiley bombs" as he subtly skewers you. Or she is habitually late or forgetful and acts as if it's *you* who has the problem. You sense that something is off-kilter, but you're not exactly sure what it is. Over time you're left with a bad taste in your mouth from the encounter or a prickly sensation of anger inside yourself. You're detecting the other person's Passive-Aggression more clearly. You find yourself becoming defensive and pulling away from contact and closeness with him or her. You've been the recipient of the Defender of the Heart known as *Passive-Aggression.*

Physician, Heal Thyself

The two of us were recently invited to a new Malibu treatment center for drug and alcohol abuse. We were excited to go for a delicious dinner and spend time reconnecting with colleagues. The evening was light-hearted, with some professional conversation; but most of the talk centered on food, dieting, and exercise (after all, this *was* Malibu!). We were sitting at a table with six other therapists, two of whom had been living together for more than 13 years. The female partner had recently lost about 60 pounds, and we commented on how beautiful and healthy she looked. Filled with great excitement and hopefulness, she told us in explicit detail about the diet she had been on for seven months and the latest Pilates class she'd gotten into.

Out of nowhere, like a dark tornado that had swept into the room, her partner spoke up with an oh-so-casual air: "I don't know how you can even subject yourself to that diet—I'd have to do something that would get me back into my 'thin' clothes faster. And isn't Pilates just stretching? . . . Guess I'm into *real* exercise." And then he topped it off by saying, "Everyone always gains the weight back anyway."

His girlfriend's face crumpled right before our eyes, and her skin seemed to lose its glow. We felt tension in the air. Talking about it the next day at the office, we shared how we'd both experienced a sickening feeling inside our stomachs at that moment. From one insensitive Passive-Aggression encounter, our initial comfort and joy at being at this event had turned into a need to flee as fast as possible. So what had happened there?

We can only surmise that our 60-pound-weight-loss friend had felt stunned and deeply wounded. She'd been speechless, unable to stand up for herself. Although you may be reading this and asking, "Why didn't she just tell him off?" it's not that easy. As is the case when anyone is hit with a passive-aggressive bomb, several things had occurred with our friend: The hostility that her partner threw at her caught her off guard. At the same time, she must have been experiencing his fury and was afraid to confront it. Most likely she knew that if she said something to stand up for herself, he would backpedal. He might have replied, "What's the matter? You're so sensitive. I only have your best interest at heart . . . blah, blah, blah." Because his aggression was so sly, she had trouble attacking it. It was like a ghost: no substance, too hard to capture.

All of us at the table took a step away from him at that moment. The irony is that we had all gone there to reconnect, and due to one passive-aggressive lob, we found ourselves totally *dis*connected. Above all, we can just imagine how much our friend had to distance *her* heart from him.

But what about her passive-aggressive partner? What must *he* have been feeling? And what prompted him to underhandedly slice and dice his girlfriend? He must have been feeling several things (hopefully, *like a jerk* was one of them); however, he couldn't discern this at that moment. So since we've known him for years and are therapists, we'll take the liberty of *telling* you what he was feeling.

We know that he was envious of his partner's weight loss, as were the rest of us at the table. We're also aware that over the past many years, his live-in partner had refused to marry him. This had left him at times with the fear that she might leave him for another man. Now, with her looking better, being admired, and feeling happy with her body and herself, it must have stirred up alarm within him. He had to have been wondering, *Will she not need me anymore? Will she fall for someone else? Did she only stay with me until she was ready to find someone better?*

All of his self-hatred and insecurity exploded in a cascade of Passive-Aggression. His anger at her, and certainly at himself, was unconscious. He's a great therapist, but you can't do brain surgery on yourself. Remember how we said that it's easier to feel someone else's Passive-Aggression than your own? This is a perfect example, especially because here was someone who is savvy, aware, and usually empathetic. His hurts and fears turned him into a passively venomous guy when his buttons were pushed.

Heart Beat

Need another reason to learn to deal openly with your anger? A long-term study from the University of Michigan suggests that having a good fight might save not just your marriage, but also your life! It appears that if both the husband and wife suppress their anger at one another when unfairly attacked, earlier death is twice as likely as in couples where one or both partners express anger and resolve the conflict. Researchers concluded that if both you and your partner tend to bury your anger, brood on it, resent one another, and avoid trying to resolve the problem, that's when *you* become an unfortunate statistic.

On this occasion, we had a ringside seat to both the passive-aggressive action and its effects on the victim. In this next instance, we only had one side of the story—Patty's. And she was dishing out Passive-Aggression like her life depended on it.

The Trickle-Down Effect

Sisterhood is sublime. It can also be the closest replication of hell on earth. Just ask Patty, a 26-year-old patient who initially came in because she loathed her work, hated dating, and was constantly annoyed with others. She'd been seeing us for five months and had been fighting a chronic "low-grade" depression for as long as she could remember.

Although Patty had started out her career with the highest hopes of becoming the best physical therapist she could be, over the past two years she had begun to dislike her patients and didn't look forward to helping them relieve their pain. To make matters worse, she recently felt "dumped" by her 24-year-old sister, Rachel. After deciding to relocate together to Los Angeles from Minneapolis two years previously, the sisters had found and moved into a gorgeous apartment. Rachel was a struggling screenwriter who paid her half of the rent by waitressing. Her social life was always hopping. She was constantly hanging out with the friends she made working at a very trendy restaurant.

Rachel often included her sister in late-night gatherings with her gang. Although Patty would go willingly, and we saw her being included as a positive, loving gesture from Rachel, she never failed to come into her therapy session and "rag" on the evening. She'd find fault with the restaurant, the food, some of the people, or her sister. And if Rachel did something without including her, Patty was sure to grouse about that, too.

The sisters had always been close since childhood, and Patty often remarked that anyone who met them thought that they were twins. Yet now Rachel hadn't been responding to Patty's recent requests to speak to their landlord together regarding the signing of a new, updated lease on their apartment.

We asked Patty about Rachel's hesitation to renew the lease. She said she didn't have a clue what the trouble was. After a few sessions of her complaining that her sister was being so immature and irresponsible, we challenged Patty to really consider why Rachel was pulling away and not stepping up to the plate. There had been no prior evidence to suggest that the younger girl was the least bit irresponsible. She'd always come through on all of her obligations. We wondered out loud if there was a link between Rachel's withdrawal and Patty's negative attitude.

Without missing a beat and with an empty smile on her lovely face, Patty tensely said, "I think I just might have to find myself therapists who really know what they're talking about."

We speculated that maybe Rachel often felt zinged and demeaned in the same way that Patty had just let *us* have it. We laid out some other situations we had observed where our patient had a way of saying one thing and meaning something else. At first Patty was speechless and looked shocked. But her next revelation brought her to tears. She started talking about Rachel, herself, and their childhood with their mother and father. We knew we'd hit pay dirt!

Patty had been injured by us. She was angry, even while maintaining that Cheshire-cat grin on her face. Momentarily, she'd felt that we were on her sister's side and we had lost sight of how she had been the victim of Rachel's flakiness. Yet at the same time, Patty was able to make a connection to what we were saying. Together, we slowly dismantled the way her family had handled their own disappointments and resentments.

In Patty and Rachel's world, rage and frustration hadn't been allowed to be met head-on. Their dad couldn't tolerate loud noises or chaos. Patty remembered her mother shushing the two girls from the time they were young when their father was around the house. She described an occasion when she and Rachel were trying to get their mom to buy them new dresses for the junior high school Valentine's Day dance. The louder they got, the more subdued Mom became. At some point in the one-sided fight, their dad came home. He stood like a stone and glared at them. Then while Mom looked scared, Dad stomped into the bedroom and shut the door. The fight was never talked about again, but this wasn't the only time that Patty and Rachel were "wordlessly" silenced.

Their parents effectively let it be known that it was unacceptable for family members to express themselves, especially when it came to unhappiness or anger. Patty and Rachel never saw their mom and dad directly confront or get upset with one another. The girls would often go to friends' houses and be amazed when *their* parents disagreed or "had words" in front of the kids.

Patty and Rachel held their parents' "calm" exteriors in high regard. Yet when asked if there was anger in the house, Patty responded, "No, but I think we felt a lot of tension." She recalled how when tensions were high, she and Rachel stayed joined at the hip, using each other as comfort against the quiet tyranny of their father.

In their house, there were also unspoken rules regarding how females were supposed to act. Being a lady meant never raising your voice and certainly never letting on that you might be upset with anyone. It also meant that you kept things congenial at all times. Mom exemplified that by being the queen "Cheshire cat." Later on in our therapy, Patty cracked up when we told her that smiling that hard is better than Botox at preventing frowns or scowls and can leave you with a permanent "nice face"!

Being brought up in a household where they had ineffectual role modeling with respect to how to deal with unpleasant, untidy feelings, the sisters never learned how to resolve differences between them. More important, they were deterred from attending to any "messy" emotions. These girls were then ripe to grab the Passive-Aggression Defender off the tree and take a big bite out of it.

Before Patty could have a decent open conversation with her sister, she needed to get familiar with the gamut of feelings she had been trying to hide from. She was quick to agree that she was very upset with Rachel for letting the lease-agreement issue continue to go unresolved. We asked her point-blank to describe how she was expressing this anger to Rachel. She realized that she wasn't letting her sister in on how upset she was, and she understood that she wasn't even allowing *herself* to be in touch with those feelings. At the same time she'd been talking negatively about Rachel to us, she'd been ignoring her sister and finding excuses not to socialize— or even be in the same room—with her.

We reminded Patty that she'd detonated a "smiley bomb" and encouraged her to be aware of the "bombs" she lobbed at Rachel and her friends. Our job was to help her sit with the discomfort that occurred inside her mind and body when she pinpointed her anger. She needed to normalize her irate feelings and learn that anger isn't something that's necessarily dangerous. In other words, she needed to begin to grow a respectful awareness of it.

There is a difference between feeling angry and acting out those angry feelings.

Patty worked hard with us to become better informed about, and sensitive to, the feelings that had been secreted away within her for so many years.

Open Sesame

If you can identify with Patty, your job now is to first unearth the anger that already lives inside you, then to understand why you've done everything you could to hide from it, and finally to comfortably coexist with it. To accomplish this tough mission, follow our three-pronged approach.

1. Cultivate Mindfulness

It's critical that you consciously nurture a keener understanding of your moods and reactions that live right under the surface. When it comes to Passive-Aggression, being better aware of your anger and hurt can mean the difference between using this mean-spirited Defender and having fully authentic and satisfying connections. To that end, we urge you to cultivate mindfulness.

In the past ten years, ancient Buddhist practices and the art of meditation have begun to permeate even middle-of-the-road, traditional psychotherapy. Although it's been 40 years since Transcendental Meditation made a huge splash when the Beatles and other '60s icons rocked it into our consciousness, meditation remained on the fringes of mainstream psychotherapy for a long time. But today, meditative practices that promote mindfulness and the art of awareness are finding a comfortable and helpful spot in our profession and in our culture at large.

Modern Western society has an overabundance of riches. It's both a blessing and a curse. We're at a point where we struggle with "too many" of everything—too many gadgets, too many choices, and too many medications that promise to fix everything—not to mention an overabundance of pain and suffering: too much materialism, too much depression, too much anxiety, too much technology that isolates us from other human beings, and too much to get done. (And, some would say, too many self-help books on the shelf telling us how to fix it all!) This overflowing, jam-packed world is so distracting that we're unable to pay close attention to our own feelings, and that's a good enough excuse to retreat from them.

Further, if Passive-Aggression is your Defender, it's only being reinforced by indirect modes of communication—such as texting, e-mailing, and social-networking Websites—that we all use to some degree or another. Even with all this pseudo-contact, significant relationships are still missing, maybe more than ever.

The most important person worth knowing and being in touch with is *you*. And the only way to really know yourself, and subsequently be connected with others, is to quiet the noise in the world around you. At the same time, you must nonjudgmentally accept the thoughts, anger, joys, obsessions, and criticisms in your head. Only then can you really begin to accept yourself, warts and all. Mindfulness is a terrific route toward a more harmonious you.

So how do you reach this state of mindfulness? As simple as it sounds, it's not that easy. It's a slow and steady process. The foundation of cultivating mindfulness is setting a time when you can sit alone daily for 10 to 15 minutes. Ideally, you should do so in a protected area somewhere in your home or out in nature where you won't be disturbed. You can have whatever you need in your sanctuary. It can be completely austere, with nothing to distract you. Alternatively, you can place items such as comfortable pillows, candles, and incense around the space to allow you to relax and experience calm. Some people even find that soft repetitive music or chants help with the process.

The idea is to free your mind and pay attention to your breathing, body, and senses. Don't try to stop the thoughts or feelings that crowd into your head, but rather just let them be there without pushing them away. If you realize that you've been preparing tonight's meal in your mind, you might find it helpful to focus on something that will hold your attention—like a candle flame or a simple mental image, such as a flower or star—that you can come back to. Alternatively, use a *mantra* (that is, a word or phrase) to help you return to a state of calm when your mind wanders. Common examples are *One* or *Peace,* or use something that's meaningful to you from your belief system. These techniques will help you gently pull yourself back to your center and to the awareness of your breath again and again.

Eventually, the voyage to just "be"—to let whatever you're feeling be okay—will get easier. And the benefits of this daily mindfulness practice last far beyond the 15 minutes you spend on it: you take it into your everyday life. Imagine if you were okay with being angry at your sister, husband, or child and gave yourself permission to feel that way? You wouldn't have a need to act it out, hide it, and hurt the other person and yourself by pretending that your feelings didn't exist. Mindfulness is a great step toward not slipping back into Passive-Aggression.

If you would like to explore the topic of mindfulness further and get some more tools for cultivating it, check out the many books, CDs, and DVDs that are devoted to this practice. A couple that we like are the book *Inner Peace for Busy People,* by Joan Z. Borysenko, Ph.D.; and its accompanying CD, *Inner Peace for Busy People: Music To Relax and Renew,* by Borysenko and Don Campbell.

2. Discover the Origins

It's essential that you explore your family of origin and other people who have left a significant impression on you in order to uncover the roots of your approach to anger. With every Defender of the Heart, you have to understand the influence of your past on your present if you want to grab hold of it and work on lessening its impact on your life. Passive-Aggression has some pretty clear-cut origins that evolve from familial ways of relating. The following are some questions that can assist you in determining if you learned to deal with anger or hurt surreptitiously or directly in your household:

- What tended to cause angry outbursts in your family?

- How did your parents convey their anger to one another and to you and your siblings?

- Who in your family set the rules when it came to how everyone dealt with this emotion?

- Did your family members tend to discharge their anger at the time it arose and then move on?

- Did they cloak their rage and allow it to simmer and smolder, only to be expressed passive-aggressively at another time?

- When someone expressed his or her anger, how did other members of the family react?

- When someone flew off the handle, what did the person say and how did he or she act?

- Did his or her behavior clear the air or cause a fire that everyone kept stoking?

- Did any member of your family frequently needle you and try to trigger your anger?

- Do you find yourself expressing your anger today in the same way that you did when you lived at home?

- Have you been exposed to different ways of expressing anger from colleagues, friends, or your partner's family?

- If you could deal with your angry feelings in any other way, what would that look like?

3. Learn to Coexist

Okay, so now you're working on developing mind-fulness, and as a result, you have a better handle on the multitude of thoughts and feelings that live inside of you. You're also more cognizant of the origins of your anger, hurt, and resentment. Bet you think that all those feelings should now up and disappear! Not so fast! They don't just take a walk. We don't know anyone who is so "Zen-ed out" that they never get their knickers in a twist!

It's not our goal to make you anger free. The aim is to get you to withstand and own your anger, coexist with it, and not let unconscious resentments leak out and poison you and those closest to you. It's how you live with your anger, what you do with it, and your ability to rule *it* rather than letting it rule *you* that's the measure of how comfortable you're becoming with those heated feelings.

Recommendations on how to deal with anger directly and not passive-aggressively have undergone a change in recent years. The old wisdom was to beat the stuffing out of a pillow or whup on a punching bag to discharge your rage. Now it's believed that those belligerent techniques only fuel it. A healthier way is to find activities that soothe your hurt heart. Certainly, you can take the route of doing something physical, but make it a joyful activity: roller-skating to music, horseback riding, swimming laps in a pool, or running with the wind in your face. You might also like to watch a gut-busting funny movie, have a good cry, or read an uplifting book. We've found, too, that assertiveness training is useful for some people.

The most effective way of dealing with your anger and pain is to straight-up talk about it with empathetic friends and colleagues and let yourself be soothed.

Here's another chance to see if Passive-Aggression is your Defender of the Heart. Mentally check off which of the following you could imagine applying to you.

Passive-Aggression Might Be Your Defender If . . .

. . . you don't have time to go to the dry cleaner's to pick up the suit your husband needs for the business trip that he says he can't take you on.

. . . you give your friend who's trying to lose weight a box of gourmet chocolate truffles for her birthday, because she's been so good on her diet that she deserves a treat.

. . . you're late for all your housing-association meetings, which wouldn't happen if they had elected *you* president and you were able to set the times.

. . . you choose bridesmaids' dresses with huge bows on the butts—they're all so skinny that they can get away with it.

. . . you cheerfully agree to work overtime when you really don't want to, then don't finish the job—how can anyone be upset when you've been so obliging?

. . . you tell your best friend that she's right about an issue even though you know she's not and will embarrass herself when she repeats her opinion to someone else.

. . . you correct your husband's grammar in public, because you wouldn't want him to make a fool of himself.

. . . you don't remind your boss about a deadline she has clearly forgotten and then sympathize with her when she gets in trouble.

. . . you drop hints that you're going to invite someone to be your date at a function, but then you don't and act surprised that the other person had that expectation.

The Payoff

Unresolved anger and hurt feelings always find a way to come back up—like acid after a bad meal—often when you least expect it. And like indigestion, this leaves you with a bitter, sour taste in your mouth and makes you feel as if you're going to choke. When these feelings surface in the form of Passive-Aggression, they may do immeasurable damage to your relationships. Side-stepping your emotions only results in a slow leakage of them onto others, making you seem like a jerk—both to those around you and to yourself—and failing to resolve the underlying problem.

But when you stop using Passive-Aggression as a device to keep yourself and loved ones at bay, contentment, satisfaction, and caring will be within your reach. And so it's up to you. The direct route is always the best and fastest path. When you decide to make peace with your feelings, you'll find resolution, either within your own heart or by reconciling with the person you have an issue with. Bringing anger to the surface, airing it in the light of day, and dealing with it appropriately allows trust to build and advances your chances of developing rich, deep relationships.

Chapter Eleven

Tell It Like It Is

"Talk Story" is an oral storytelling tradition from Hawaii that we like a lot. We're finishing up the book with a chapter of narratives from some celebrities and show-biz personalities to show how telling your own story is a great way to help you get to the root of your own Defenders of the Heart.

It's been said that the only difference between a rut and a grave is the depth. Some of us spend years buried in ruts we've made for ourselves with our Defenders. A great way to start breaking out of these self-imposed limitations is to recognize them for what they are: defensive routines that we get into early in life and that don't change until we become conscious of them. You've read this book, and now you have some appreciation of the Defenders you employ on a regular basis. Telling your story to a receptive friend or family member, or by forming a "Talk Story" group, can help you further see how your unconscious Defenders hold you back from fully embracing the entirety of you life: emotionally, socially, and intellectually.

Setting out to tell your story might seem a bit overwhelming, not to mention intimidating, at first. Rather than trying to recount your entire personal history from birth, start out by thinking of some important life event or connection with a significant person. You'll get the idea from reading the Talk Stories in this chapter.

If you have trouble getting started, first do the relaxation exercise we gave you in Chapter 1 or the mindfulness technique in the last chapter.

When you tell your story to others, set some guidelines. There should be no interrupting, criticizing, or judging. Most important, there should be no pressure to reveal anything that you don't want to talk about. Don't bother trying to make your story grammatically correct or worry about your "style." Just talk in a natural, conversational way.

Be prepared to listen to other people's stories, too. You might be able to identify with them, or they could inspire you or touch you in ways you wouldn't have expected. It might also be easier to identify Defenders when you see them in action in another. Sometimes you find yourself getting upset or angry with those who reflect traits and behaviors that you dislike in yourself.

While sharing your story with a sympathetic listener in a safe environment can be an enriching experience that can help you delve further into your Defenders, you might not be ready to take this step. An alternative is to write your story in your journal or on your computer and share it only when you're ready to do so. We believe that it's better if you write your story by hand—somehow this seems to offer closer proximity to your heart, without being distanced by a technical apparatus. But of course, many people are attuned to using keyboards, so if that's the way you feel most comfortable, go ahead and type it out.

Now read the stories we were privileged to hear, which we share with you in the pages that follow. Some people overcame their Defenders of the Heart to lead full and productive lives. Others harnessed them and transformed them into a beneficial resource. As you're reading, see if you can identify who overcame, and who positively harnessed, their Defenders of the Heart. We give you *our* analysis of how they did so at the end of each story. (By the way, none of these people were ever our patients, but were very generous in sharing their stories with us for this book.)

Ryan Seacrest

Ryan Seacrest is the host of the blockbuster TV show *American Idol.* He also hosts *On-Air with Ryan Seacrest,* a popular morning drive-time show on L.A.'s KIIS-FM, and *American Top 40,* syndicated on the nation's top radio stations; has hosted the Emmys; and was voted one of the "50 Most Beautiful" stars by *People* magazine, among a myriad of other achievements.

A famous, rich, and good-looking guy with one of the biggest hit shows on television, Ryan seems to have mastered life. But like all of us, he has faced his share of hardships. He's a great example of someone who has beaten adversity to achieve his ultimate goal: becoming a celebrity. However, it did come with costs. These days he has a better understanding of what drives him and how to handle failure when it occurs.

On the morning we met with him, Ryan received some tough news: a daytime-television talk show he'd been involved with had been canceled after a single season.

"I've got a lot on my plate right now. It's been a disappointing day. But what's happened to me this morning has helped me focus and get clearer. I know what I want to talk about regarding my Defender of the Heart. Interestingly enough, a defense I used early on in my life is helping me today to put perspective on what I'm going through now.

"I grew up in Atlanta, Georgia. My parents were pretty conventional. We had a nice house—not that extravagant, but hey, we had a two-car garage. And I couldn't imagine that I could ever in my life pay a mortgage for a house with a two-car garage.

"When I was 12 years old, I knew something about myself that not too many kids my age knew. I had already made my mind up about what I wanted to do with my life. No matter what the cost, somehow, somewhere, I knew I wanted to be around radio stations, and maybe even TV.

"As a kid, I was always very active. You know, I wasn't the kid who could just raise my hand and keep quiet in class. I was the kid who had tons of energy, aggressiveness, and a drive to make myself known. That passion, along with a youthful fierceness, was apparently what gave me the courage to leave my family behind and move to the West Coast.

"That burning desire I started to feel at age 12 never left me. At 19, it burned even hotter. I realized that my hometown wasn't big enough for the goals in my mind. I remember the evening so clearly when

I went to my folks and said, 'I've got to try something. I have to try because I can't rest. I'm going to move to L.A. to pursue what I believe is my path.'

"My parents were shocked. I knew they had a monumental decision to make: either they were going to support me or we would all be fighting for a long time to come. Looking back on it now, my parents were in a tough spot. It's a fine balance in supporting the passions of a child who's chasing a very difficult dream, but at the same time making sure that there is some kind of pragmatic reality for your child to hold on to. My parents supported my dreams emotionally, but I existed mostly on cereal in L.A. for some time. Sushi was only in my fantasies!

"I've lived here now for ten years. But I remember those years of struggle like it was yesterday—starting off knowing no one, driving a van for a radio station. Every inch, foot, and yard of progress I made was designed to get me one step closer to where I wanted to be. I wasn't about to go home with my tail between my legs. And I was scared to death. I kept my mind on my passion and what I needed to do. I'd identified this dream, and I wasn't about to listen to people around me who were constrained. There was no way I would hear anything that would interfere.

"Most of us are conditioned to think we can't achieve our dreams. I think it's a blessing that I knew so early in my life there was nothing else that would fulfill me except this pursuit. And there was nothing else I was going to do.

"Even though there is a part of me that feels bummed and discouraged today on the cancellation of the TV show, a bigger part of me realizes I can't go there. For me, life is all about identifying a desire, a *passion, and going for it with all my energy. Although it failed, <u>we</u> didn't really fail. <u>I</u> didn't really fail. It was something I wanted. I tried. I went for it. A passion was identified and completed. Success is what you find in the process of working toward a dream, not necessarily just in the successful outcome.*

"Hey, I know I'm lucky! I got a great opportunity with <u>American Idol.</u> But even without that break, I'm still that kid who would be working somewhere in TV or radio. My desire always had to do with being out there in the media some way. And I would do it in any shape or form, because I love it.

"Funny, but the foundation of <u>American Idol</u> is all about this lesson. Here are kids from all over the country who believe in a dream, have passion. Each one gives it his or her all, although only some of them come out with recording contracts and millions of bucks. But ultimately they are all successful. They have a dream and they follow it through. Some get more rewards than others, but in the long run, like me, they listened to their passion and went for it!"

Ryan began a step ahead of many people who struggle to reach almost insurmountable goals. From an early age, he had his eye on the prize; no matter the heartache or failures he went through, he found a way to bear it. Ryan's been a pro since childhood in using his Defender of the Heart—Denial—to his advantage. He knew as a kid that the only career he wanted was on radio or TV. In adulthood, he clearly sees now that he was eager and felt invincible in his youth. He recognizes that he pushed down intolerable feelings of fear of failure in this highly competitive field. He simply put all his doubts and fears into a mental basket and did any job he could with great fervor. This protected him from the pain suffered along his journey, and he kept moving ahead to success.

Today Ryan can see how driven he was and how he needed to dampen down his fearful feelings in pursuit of a level of success that was almost impossible to achieve. Even with this particular day's big disappointment, he was able to put it into perspective and not let it cripple him.

Ryan has learned over time that a pinch of Denial helps him keep going and stay on track. He's grateful for his successes, keeps his failures in perspective, and uses his Defender of the Heart more consciously than in his youth.

Our interview with Ryan reveals that the important thing is learning how to deal with our underlying emotions consciously, not automatically, so we are able to piece together the right solution to each puzzle that life gives us. Ryan is a perfect example of someone who used Denial in a way that served him well in his professional pursuits. Defenders of the Heart can certainly be helpful, not always harmful. In the career that Ryan chose, the odds greatly favor failure over success. In order for him to keep going despite the inevitable pitfalls, Denial was a strong option.

Wendie Jo Sperber

Wendie Jo Sperber died of breast cancer at the age of 47. Shortly before her death, we had the honor of meeting with her to talk about her life and her life's work. For those of you who would know a face on television but not necessarily a name, Wendie was an actress who achieved a high level of recognition when she starred with Tom Hanks and Peter Scolari in the '80s sitcom *Bosom Buddies.* She went on to act in many other TV shows, such as *Will & Grace* and *8 Simple Rules;* and she also had roles in numerous movies, including the *Back to the Future* films.

We joined Wendie at a bright storefront office called weSPARK in the San Fernando Valley, outside of L.A. It was filled with calm colors, comfortable couches, and a lot of people milling around with cheerful faces. You might not expect such a warm and joyful feeling when walking into a support center geared toward cancer patients and their families, but it was alive and pulsating with activity and positive energy. Here was a place that not only offered supportive group counseling for those with cancer, but also for kids, teens, spouses, and the caregivers touched by the disease. It also provides informational seminars, arts and crafts, movement and music, and huge hugs and hand-holding. And Wendie was the catalyst for this oasis. We wanted to hear directly from her what had prompted her to take her health crisis and turn it into something meaningful and necessary for the community.

"You should know what the name weSPARK stands for," Wendie said. She told us that she originally wanted the word *SPARK*—standing for Support, Prevention, Acceptance, Recovery, and Knowledge—but the acronym was already taken, so she added the little *we* before it. "After all, we all get together here, and we all have a light that shines." So weSPARK was born.

"Words destroyed my self-confidence and left a lasting effect on how I defined myself by the sixth

grade. Walking home from school, a girl called me fat. I went home and looked at myself. Look at the picture of my daughter at that age. [At this point, Wendie showed us a photo of her lovely ten-year-old.] *I looked just like that—not fat, just round and cute. But I told myself at age 11, I guess that's what fat looks like. And it's been a battle within me ever since. I think words scarred me forever—words that made me feel bad, unlovable, untouchable, everything—words I never made peace with.*

"*Now jump to my being diagnosed with cancer in June '97. Listen to this: I'm told I have cancer, and my first thought is, Oh good, I'll get chemo and lose a lot of weight. Not Oh my God, I have cancer! How nuts is that?*

"*At first it was early detection, so no big deal. But the words affect you; they really do. They leave you thinking about yourself in another way—a way that is all about death, hair loss, and sickness. And other people see you through their keyhole of what cancer means to them.*

"*I had a double mastectomy when the spot was first discovered. But then two years ago, I found the cancer had spread to my lung and bone. And now I've been doing chemo for the past year—every day for two weeks and then off for a week.*

"*I miss the old Wendie. I have no energy. My hands and feet are so blistered, and I miss dancing and walking in the canyon. Remember, everyone has words to describe this, and it keeps them removed from you and the disease. It's such a lonely thing. This guy I really loved and who loved me couldn't take it after a year and left. He really couldn't* understand what was going on. At the time I had a very young daughter who worried that she was going to 'catch it.'

"It hit me that there was no place for her to go, no other kids to talk to and hang with who understood what it was like to have a mom with this illness. There were support places, but they didn't seem to cater to the very young, and most women who went there were much older than I was. For God's sake, there are over two million people here in the Valley, and there was nothing for us. So after trying to be involved with a bunch of different places, I decided, _You know what? I'm just gonna do this myself._ My cousin had just died of leukemia, and her family had no right place for them or her to go before she died.

"Originally I did everything, and, of course, I didn't pay myself. Now everyone is doing the jobs I did, and thank God. I still do a lot of fund-raising, and that helps us so much. With my health the way it has been, I unfortunately have to take a backseat, and that is so tough for me to do.

"There is a great energy here, and it's a community that is growing by leaps and bounds. You know, I look around and laugh. Just a few months before I was diagnosed, I sort of said, 'I'm done; I've had it with acting.' I was just bored and felt there was something more I needed to do. Then I got the cancer verdict. And quitting acting was out because I have to work to keep up my health insurance!

"But this has become my world and my life in a very different way than acting. This is so very powerful. One little seed and look what has blossomed. Everybody does so much, and there is so much

*understanding here. I've learned to let the harsh
words go, even the mean ones inside myself."*

When we learned that Wendie had passed away, our
thoughts and prayers went out to her kids and family.
But we also knew that because of her Altruism, thousands
of individuals and families would continue to reap the
rewards of her devotion. This Defender is like a snow-
ball: it starts with a small flake and gains substance and
momentum as it goes, impacting generations to come.
With that one word, *cancer,* Wendie began a painful journey that has forever touched the lives of so many.

Patrick Dempsey

Patrick Dempsey is the star and vibrant sex symbol
of the hit prime-time TV show *Grey's Anatomy.* Now in
his early 40s, he has been starring in movies and television since he was a teenager.

When we had our morning interview with Patrick,
we asked him to speak about the time in his life when
people in the entertainment industry were cold and dismissive of him, despite previous successes. Luckily for
women around the world, he ultimately landed his current role as "Dr. McDreamy" and has gone on to star on
the big screen, too.

He arrived an hour late for our breakfast meeting,
but it was hard for us to be miffed: it's difficult to bear
a grudge against such a kind, handsome guy, especially
when he explained that his baby had thrown up and
he'd had to help his wife.

"I grew up in Buckfield, Maine. I was an athletic kid who got hooked on performing after placing second in the International Jugglers competition. After that, I knew that the theater was the place for me, so I dropped out of high school at 17 to try my luck in the big city: New York. I remember seeing my dad in the door frame when I left the house on my way to the train station. I got a strange feeling at that moment that my adolescence was literally over.

"I had just been in New York a short time, trying to get used to the big city, when my dad died. At a time when I needed a great male role model, I was truly all alone. I had no father to lean on, to talk to, and to unearth his wisdom for me. I was really on my own, and I was still a kid.

"Almost immediately I was cast in the Broadway show _Torch Song Trilogy._ This was the early '80s, coming from a little town to the big city, and it all came so easy.

"Ignorance was bliss. If I'd known how much unemployment and rejection goes with the life of an actor, I might never have had the guts to do this.

"As my early success grew, I was surrounded by people who had become bitter with the struggle to get work and to make a name for themselves in show business. I felt a sense of guilt over my success. Some of these actors even had success for a time and then lost it. Little did I know that _I_ would be in their place very soon.

"Heading into my mid-20s, I had a strong film career going. But with more attention being paid to me, I started to doubt that my acting abilities were completely solid. Tied in to that doubt was the realization that this profession was my job and my livelihood—I really couldn't do anything else. I needed to figure out a way to quell these self-doubts. I began to study with a lot of great teachers. I was attracted to the teachers who gave me the power to make choices on my own, not those who told me how to do it.

"Coincidentally, at the same time I was starting to question myself, I was also beginning a ten-year cycle of being out of favor with producers and casting directors. For a time I got offered everything, like I was the wonder boy. Suddenly, I was going into rooms filled with producers, directors, and casting people who—because I may not have fit their bill—were either blasé or chock-full of animosity.

"So, now what? I'd had this great run. I'd met all my goals and exceeded my expectations. I became depressed. I thought that being a successful working actor was a goal that would give me a sense of who I was. Now I realized that I had no new goals to meet. I'd gotten sidetracked and was just drifting. I didn't know what these new goals should be. I only knew that I was beginning to understand that the outside world wasn't gratifying to me. I thought that maybe something inside me needed to shift.

"Especially between the ages of 25 and 32, life was really tough for me . . . all those auditions, those failed hopes for work. I worried that I'd become like those embittered actors I'd met when I was on the rise: someone who lived his life grumbling about lost opportunities. At the same time, I started to notice that I was losing the arrogance of youth. I was discovering my flaws, and that shook me up. My *confidence was really faltering. If I wasn't defined by who was going to hire me, could I find my self-worth and value within myself? After all, the teachers and mentors I seemed to be most drawn to were those who inspired me to figure out the world for myself.*

"Ever since leaving home at 17, my dream was to return to Maine someday a success, and find a home of my own. This was as good a time as any, success or not. My mom had just been diagnosed with cancer. I was in a blossoming relationship with my soon-to-be wife. And my acting career sucked.

"We found an old ship captain's home that needed a lot of work. Ironically, through rebuilding this old home with my mom's help, she and I were also able to reconstruct a relationship that had been strained for years. We were able to forge a new adult connection. I was no longer just her kid. This time when I would get ready again to leave Maine and seek my fame and fortune, I would no longer be that naïve 17-year-old boy.

"As my Maine home took shape, so did I. It was becoming clearer that I was who I was, looked the way I looked, sounded the way I sounded. I was making peace with that. I continued searching deep down inside myself for what I thought and felt. I sought more understanding through my friends, mentors, and therapy. I was realizing that if I only put energy into getting the next acting job, I would have nothing else to pull from. I would remain rudderless and depressed.

"I needed to believe in myself. I needed a life with a loving partner, a life with other passions besides this fickle business. I needed a life with meaning for

me. *I was more painfully aware that acting was my
choice for life. I needed it not only to fill my pockets
but also to feed my soul. I needed it for sustenance,
but I knew that I couldn't be a slave to it.*

*"Twenty years before, my dad had stood at the
door of our home bidding me good-bye. He had faith
in my abilities and my character. It took that long for
me to have faith in myself. With his wisdom that was
gone too soon, he allowed me to come full circle—to
pursue the dream that would feed my heart and to
grow into the man he believed I would become."*

Patrick experienced tough times—not only in leaving home so young and confronting the tragic loss of his father in his late teens, but also when his flourishing career hit a wall. After finally coming to a profound understanding that his profession was as important to him as the air he breathed, he was thwarted from using that passion. To help steer himself through it, he depended on his healthy Defender, Sublimation.

Using Sublimation, Patrick learned that he could be self-reliant during his greatest disappointments. Patrick chose to focus his unused creativity into another creative space. By going back to his childhood home, beginning a restoration project, rebuilding an adult connection with his mother, and being fully invested in the relationship with his future bride, he used his Defender wisely. He didn't allow this part of his life to overtake and replace what he knew he desired to do as a career. But he used Sublimation judiciously by channeling his disappointments and frustrations into other forms of expression.

Through years filled with the highest of highs and the lowest of lows—leaving home at an early age, losing his father in adolescence, and going from superstardom to rock bottom—Patrick unearthed the ability to look inward and find his power. Because at that time in his life he was able to open up to mentors and loved ones and in therapy, his heart was less defended and he was freer with his feelings. This helped him absorb a difficult stretch and not let it defeat him.

Warren Bell

Warren Bell is a successful writer/producer of television sitcoms. He's been an executive producer on such hits as *According to Jim, Ellen,* and *Coach;* and he also wrote a number of episodes for those shows. He's a member of the board of directors of the Corporation for Public Broadcasting and is a contributor to *National Review Online.* Given his facility for storytelling, Warren kept us enthralled with his harrowing tale when we sat down with him. He's married and a dad to two young boys, neither of whom was yet born at the time these events occurred.

"I experienced an event in my life some years ago that actually touched me greatly, but I didn't come to recognize its powerful effect on my life until much later.

"It's spring 1993, and I've just finished my third year in the TV business. I'm a producer on the hit series <u>Coach.</u>

"Although I'm a guy who doesn't get riled very easy, a guy who seems to be pretty even-keeled, it's been a tough and volatile set, and I'm glad the

season has come to an end. I'm at the wrap party at Dodger Stadium, and one of the writers, Bill, who has become a friend, invites me to join him and 15 other guys for a fishing expedition: male bonding! I don't have too much time to get excited because we're waking up bright and early the very next day to catch the 45-foot boat, a big one that sleeps 12.

"Driving home that night, my wife, Lee, says, 'I just have this sense that tomorrow's boat trip is the beginning of a bad TV movie. You know, 15 writers get into a boat and head out to sea. . . .' I have to chuckle.

"The next morning after boarding the boat at the marina, we head out to sea. It's beautiful. Dolphins are running with us, seals swimming by; even my seasickness can't mar the gorgeous day. Our captain and the first mate take us out far enough to start fishing. Not being a great fisherman, I prefer to sit in the sun, drink a beer or two, and just enjoy the sea.

"After we fish and relax, the plan is to cruise out to Santa Barbara Island, a small island that's a state park. We'll anchor about 100 yards off the island, take a rubber dinghy ashore, picnic, and hike around the park. The weather is great: about 60 or 65 degrees. There's a little chop in the water but nothing too serious.

"I can see a volcanic-looking island with few trees and no sign of a beach or dock. There's a metal ladder that comes down off a cliff into a small rocky cove. I realize that the only way to reach the island is to navigate the rubber dinghy close to the ladder, grab on to it, and climb up 40 feet.

"So Bill and I, along with another friend, Eric, decide to take the dinghy out first. We start heading toward the island, and some waves start coming up. The closer we get to the rocks, the more waves seem to be picking up behind us—now they're about three to four feet high. I'm starting to wonder how we're going to make this happen. Bill's sitting in the back steering the dinghy, Eric's in the front, and I'm in the middle. We approach the metal ladder much faster than we thought we would, and Bill yells to Eric to grab it. But we're going at least five miles an hour in this increasingly rough ocean, and there is no way Eric can get hold! So we're in this little dinghy, surfing on good-sized waves, and we're heading into a bunch of jagged rocks!

"The dinghy crashes into the first rock and folds in half. Eric and Bill are immediately thrown out of the raft. I'm still hanging on in the middle, with the front of the boat butted up against my face. The dinghy and I are in front of a huge wall of rocks, and I'm freaking out with the thought of more waves thrashing me against their sharp points. The only thing I think of doing to save myself from that fate is to get out of the middle of the boat. Of course, that effort lands me smack in the water, with the boat going in another direction. Trying to grab on to slick volcanic rock is like grabbing a handful of wet razor blades.

"I end up chest deep in water at the mouth of a cave that maybe goes back 60 feet. As the waves crash against me, I turn into a pinball inside this cave, falling down underwater and then resurfacing for air. Because the surf and undertow are so rough, I can't swim out to the ladder about 40 feet away. I'm trying to hold on to rock and stand on sand that is sucking me under. I hit my head really hard against a rock. I can't keep treading water when the waves come in. I throw off my leather jacket because it's too heavy and cold. I am thoroughly exhausted. I'm 29 years old. I've been married for only six months. And I realize that I'm going to die.

"Meanwhile, Bill and Eric have been able to get on top of the cave. They've been trying to reach out for me, but they are at least ten feet above me, and they must see me tossed in and out of the cave like a rag doll. Even though I feel hopeless, I continue to struggle to survive.

"A new thought comes from somewhere inside me, a new feeling, perhaps a voice—I'm not sure. But inside myself I hear my thoughts, which say: <u>I need to get out of here because Lee is pregnant. There's a baby waiting for me.</u> Now my wife had just taken a pregnancy test that had come out negative, but something inside me says I have to get through this; someone is waiting.

"At the same time I feel this inner force, I'm also aware that as I go farther inside the cave, I'm more protected and I can get above the water level. Ultimately, I can rest on dry land. Now I know I won't drown . . . just die of starvation!

"So maybe 15 minutes pass, and I'm sitting, freezing cold and exhausted. I hear Bill's voice: 'Warren . . . Warren, are you in there? Can you swim out?'

"I tell him, 'Yeah, that's why I'm just sitting here!'

"As luck or God would have it, the park rangers change shifts every two weeks, and guess what? This is that day. A boat just happens to show up, and 12 guys with rock-climbing equipment and scuba suits are here. My cave has a chimney opening that goes up to the top. It's very narrow, but I try finding hand- and footholds to get up far enough for the guys to get a rope down the chimney and around me. Maybe there is always that reserve of strength in all of us; I don't know. Maybe it's something bigger than I am; I don't know. But finally I'm on the top of the rocks, and a Coast Guard helicopter comes and lowers a basket for me. Bill also goes up in a basket because he, too, has been injured trying to help the divers get to me.

"We fly to a hospital nearby. In the helicopter I'm thinking, <u>I should be scared, but I'm not.</u> I'm thinking, <u>Bring it on,</u> like that movie <u>Fearless</u> about a fatal plane crash. I've been through this, and nothing can kill me now. I get stitches in my head, stitches in my elbows, and I'm bruised a lovely shade of purple from head to toe.

"Between the beating I'd endured and the pain pill I'd taken, I'm sleeping deeply when my wife awakens me at 6 A.M. with her crying. She's taken a pregnancy test and it's positive. I'm elated! In the next few days, I remember my thoughts in that cave. I remember knowing inside myself that I needed to get out alive, that someone not here yet would be counting on me to make it out.

"I turn 30. I become a first-time father. And I live with that near-death event daily. I take a risk by quitting a well-paying job. I notice I'm paying atten- tion to feelings like I've never paid attention to them before. Remember, I am the guy who is seemingly unaffected by the ups and downs of life. But now, in finally paying attention to my feelings that I have *ignored for most of my life, I recognize something profound: I've been living my entire life surrounded by a halo of depression. For my own personal reasons, I've been squelching my joys, fears, and excitements to hide them from myself.*

"I realize more and more as the days pass how short life is. Although I can't state with certainty that my almost-death experience left me a changed man, my behaviors seem to be acknowledging it."

As we listened to Warren tell this riveting tale, we were struck by the fact that he didn't see himself as someone who had been dramatically changed by a traumatic event. He did, however, recognize the gutsy choices he made to leave a financially secure job even with the upcoming birth of his first child. His thinking became crystal clear on how he had lived his life up until the boating accident: detached from most of his feelings, numbed to his joys and fears by a life that was framed by depression.

For many years, Warren had used the written word and his creative brain to make a good living for himself. While his Intellectualization worked well for him, it also kept him at a distance from his deeper feelings. His terrifying, life-threatening ordeal allowed him to become more attuned to the Defenders he had placed around his heart. He uncovered more of himself and began his journey to become a man who lived not only with his brain but also with his heart.

We can only speculate that Warren's intuition in that cave about his unborn child could be attributed to two things: First, there are things that none of us really knows but which we can only hope; there is something out there bigger than us that we can tap into for comfort and guidance. Second, Warren could be speaking about his own inner voice that was yearning for him to grow and develop beyond where he was at that time in his life.

Mary Lynn Rajskub

Mary Lynn Rajskub, an actress in her mid-30s, costars as computer genius Chloe O'Brian opposite Kiefer Sutherland on the long-running hit show *24.* She's also worked on a number of popular films, including *Sweet Home Alabama, Legally Blonde 2,* and *Little Miss Sunshine.*

One Sunday afternoon, Mary Lynn sat down with us in her sunny, work-in-progress, dog-filled home to relay her Talk Story. Her *life* was currently a work in progress, too, as she was at that time expecting her first child.

Mary Lynn opened up to us and shared the journey that got her from her hometown of Trenton, Michigan, to Los Angeles and eventually onto an award-winning TV show. What struck us right away was her early desire to take a different path from that of her family. In hindsight, she could now see how she'd craved to set herself apart from them. At the time, however, she had very little conscious awareness of this at all. She almost took the course that would see her marrying young, staying local, and never gracing a stage. Some steady, persistent, almost unconscious drive kept turning her away from "settling."

> *"I had fear and guilt thinking and feeling separately from what my family thought and felt. When I was a child, I worked hard at having no expression*

on my face so that no one would know what I was thinking and feeling. If you ask anyone who knew me then, they'd say I wasn't a funny kid. Funny how 'being funny' became my job later on.

"I guess I knew early on I just had to move away to be myself. Thinking about it now, I realize how my mom recognized from my high school interest in theater and fine arts that I needed to be stimulated, that I needed to do creative things. She and my dad set me up in a watercolor art class at a local strip mall. I remember painting watercolor flowers, like greeting cards. I knew that college was out for me; I wanted to go to art school. And I did, and it was eye-opening and wonderful.

"No one in my family had gone to college. I paid for it all by putting school on my charge card. I think I went there not only for the love of art, but because of the fear of staying stuck forever in an unchallenging job. Maybe with that in my mind, when my best friend asked me to join her for a semester in San Francisco, I jumped at the chance. I think I knew somewhere inside that I was going to be there for much longer.

"San Francisco is where I got into performance art. And then somehow I was making fun of it, and the lines got blurry. I was doing comedy. I was getting laughs. Or was I being laughed _at_ first? However it started, I got cast in a live comedy show. I suppose I did comedy out of a need to express myself. So much of my humor was born out of my own nervousness and being uncomfortable. It was real and it was funny, and I knew I could craft an act and keep doing it even when the nerves finally left me. I liked what

I was doing. I was gaining security and confidence. I decided that I had nothing to lose . . . might as well move to Los Angeles.

"I noticed when I moved here, a lot of people had a chip on their shoulder. You know, they were negative and had a 'The world is against me' kind of attitude. We all weren't talking about any kind of faith, spirituality, or any real feelings whatsoever. Then I had a devastating breakup of a relationship. I knew that I needed to start thinking about how to keep positive when things go wrong. I started to use that pain to open myself up to exploring my spirituality. I went on auditions and really began to examine myself so that I could express myself in the best way I knew how.

"Now, with my newfound success, my growing security in myself, and my ability to better understand myself, I'm able to be more present. I'm able to see the gifts I have, work hard for them, and know that I can set my mind to do things. Even if things I try don't work out, hey, that's all right—I'll try something else. Writing, painting, performing, directing my 'Webisodes' on MySpace: it's all creative to me. I know I'll always work at being creative.

In childhood, Mary Lynn was a master of keeping her emotions hidden from view. We speculate that she used that trusty Defender of the Heart, Denial, at this early time in her life. She protected herself from those terrifying conflicting feelings of wanting to be separate from, yet needing connection to, her family; she denied them to herself and to others.

As she moved away from home, she found the need to continue to perform. What she didn't realize was that the Humor she displayed at her own nervous expense became a Defender that protected her from her discomfort and unease. Not only did it buffer her from the anxiety of being out in front of an audience, but it softened the blow of having done things differently from her family of origin as well.

We hypothesize that Mary Lynn probably turned to her deadpan Humor before she even reached a performing arena. Initially, this Defender protected her from feelings that were unbearable: separation, fear of rejection, embarrassment, and isolation. With time, she was able to manage this Defender and use it to her advantage, knowing when, and when not, to call upon it. Her Defender still works for her today, but her awareness of herself allows her to be in the driver's seat of her life.

Joe Crummey

Joe Crummey is a radio talk-show host in his early 50s who was a fixture in Southern California for more than 30 years before becoming just as popular in Phoenix, Arizona. Joe has always had a loyal following and is known for his irreverent wit and topical, conservative stance. He's a sarcastic and right-to-the-point kind of guy when it comes to the callers on his show, yet when it came to being as clear with himself, it was once a different story. He realized there were a lot of consistent reasons why his career and his love life were going in circles. He was a master of Rationalization . . . until he couldn't master it anymore.

"I really lived a life of Peter Pan. I was single, moving around in a succession of jobs as a disc jockey. Take life seriously? Are you nuts? The most serious thing I had to deal with was getting up earlier than most people because of my early-morning deejaying. I always seemed to get by. I was the center of the universe. Life was great. I was having a good time.

"In 1993 I was working in a TV station in San Diego. And the weirdest thing—I thought, <u>Here I am fitted with these customized earpieces designed specifically for each reporter's ears, and they're not working so good. And to boot, they're giving me a headache. This cheap, crappy station!</u>

"Shoot to 1994, and I'm back in the big-radio market—Los Angeles—on the number one talk-radio station. Life is good, but I'm still having those damn headaches, still not hearing so great, even in this state-of-the-art studio. I sure as hell know it's not the equipment this time, but I'm equally sure it has to do with the loud music I've been listening to all these years. On the recommendation of a close friend who had some ear problems and headaches, I get myself to the House Ear Institute.

"Life can fall apart very fast. The doctor there, unemotional, announces, 'Oh, you've got a brain tumor. You'll most likely lose your hearing. We're worried about your facial nerve that runs right through there and controls your smile and whether or not you'll be able to close your eyes. If it goes bad, we can always tape your eyes open.'

"What the hell?!

"I gotta be on the air tomorrow morning. <u>This is somebody else's chart here—sorry, buddy.</u> This is not *good. And it's a very tough four days from Wednesday's news to surgery Monday morning. No one else can help me. I'm really alone. They say I have no choice: I'll die if I don't do this, even if this thing isn't malignant. My life is crashing.*

"Friday before surgery I'm driving home from the radio station. I look into the rearview mirror and see a face that was sorta familiar to me. I hadn't seen that face in 30 or 40 years. It was <u>my</u> face: the face of a kid crying.

"So Monday morning I'm all doped up for surgery. And now I don't give a damn about anything. I'm lying on this skinny table, it's freezing, and I'm a piece of meat. And I don't care. And at the last moment, I'm not concerned about dying—I'm concerned about my living: what if I can't function?

"So I wake up and I'm in hell. When they break your head open, it's not such a good idea. I had double vision and was so dizzy. In removing my brain tumor, they destroyed the ear canal. Nobody told me I'd have to relearn how to stand and walk again without falling over and puking. Nobody told me that my friends would come to visit and not know where to look, as if I had cooties. You know damn well they feel relief because it isn't them. And they say things like 'Think positive' and how 'lucky' I am. And I want to scream back at them, 'If I was so lucky, I wouldn't have this damn thing in the first place!' Support helps, but all the positive attitude sometimes just doesn't cut it.

"I've lost something big—my immortality. I never thought I was going to die. I never thought anything bad would really happen to me. I thought I would go through life avoiding pain very well, avoiding my

life very well. I was always good at making excuses for everything. You know, I sought pleasure—always. Don't we all? But always running to pleasure is really to avoid life's pain.

"Within a matter of weeks, I got back to work. Somehow I realized I was still here on this planet. But it was different. I couldn't stand where I was. I was living with reminders: my deafness, my balance, my awareness of my physical pain, healing. My life had abruptly changed.

"My life also started to change in gradual ways. I was starting to see other people's pain, too. The more I was living my regular life, the more my old life was becoming irregular. I was the guy who joked about others' pain. We all do that sometimes. Now I was the guy who had to come face-to-face with <u>his</u> pain. Nobody wants to look at their pain. Hey, I don't blame anyone—I don't. But I can't pretend life is just a cakewalk anymore. And that's a good thing: not to find reasons to avoid living my life.

"And my job? Talk radio. The job is looking different to me. I hate to say it, but my always being the jokester, not seeing talk radio as serious and something I loved, was a way for me to devalue something I really cared about.

"My girlfriend of many years who'd been bugging me to get married looked like good marriage material. I'm now committed to my wife, and we have a four-year-old kid: a son. I look at my son—it all revolves around him; he thinks it's about him all the time. That used to be me. It all revolved around me. The truth is, I'm a really small point in the universe. Now I know what's really changed. I revolve around others: my wife, my son, my listeners. I worry now about my son. My grip on life I know is tenuous. I worry about his safety like I never worried about anyone before. And it's good to be unselfish, but it's a burden—a good burden. When he was an infant, I carried him everywhere in a sling. He was protected by me all the time. He's growing; it's hard to protect him from everything now.

"Everything about this stupid brain tumor has helped me with every single thing, every day. It helps me with my job, my son, and my relationship. I feel different about the world, and I feel different about people in it. I understand their pain; and what's so cool, this may sound pompous, but I can put myself in their shoes.

"You spend your life avoiding this stuff—heartache, pain, loss, and grief. I get it. That's what we've been doing since we came out of the chute: we want to avoid pain. In my life, if I let someone else in, it would become a part of my pain, too, and I wasn't about to do that. So I found excuses to avoid feelings. And I don't do that anymore. Tolerating my feelings helped me find my humanity. With my wife, when I can't stand to hear her one more moment, I remember I'm deaf on one side and I haven't been listening.

"As for my son, I worry now more for him than myself. The lesson I learned and the lesson I'm still learning every day . . . the greater the pain of being alive, the greater the goddamn benefit!"

Joe learned a valuable lesson about himself from a painful, life-threatening event: he learned that he'd been avoiding "growing up," that he'd been self-centered. Joe's wake-up call found him with the realization that there was more to life than just "Joe." He hadn't been committing to his long-term girlfriend, to his work, to his health and well-being, and to the reality that life doesn't go on forever.

With the advent of his brain tumor, Joe's Defender of the Heart was dismantled quickly when he was faced with the possibility of looming death. Prior to this health crisis, Joe lived a life shrouded in Rationalization—his tried-and-true defense. When he wouldn't get the job he yearned for or things weren't 100 percent perfect in his relationship, he'd diminish his feelings of despair or disappointment by shrugging them off. He'd rationalize how he knew "that job" wasn't the right one for him anyway. He'd find a way to remain uncommitted in his relationship—not getting in or out, comfortable in staying stuck.

Coming to grips with the fact that life is finite and fragile, Joe became *un*stuck and was able to move into adulthood. With this growing up, Joe's life became more enriched, his relationship more meaningful, and his purpose on Earth more defined. He is "marked" forever by his hearing loss. When he falls back to his old patterns—his comfortable Rationalizations—he's among the lucky ones; he has something that reminds him of his continuing lesson: that there is more to life than Joe.

We hope the preceding Talk Stories were inspiring and thought provoking. Perhaps they offered a small

window into how other people—some you may have admired from afar, and some you've just been introduced to—have come around to paying attention to their Defenders.

Our profound hope is that with the help of this book, you will also start paying attention to *yours*. Further, we trust that these Defenders of the Heart have gone from just being words we all throw around in conversation to now being meaningful concepts that you can recognize and employ in your quest for a richer, more satisfying life!

AFTERWORD

In these pages we've introduced you to ten Defenders of the Heart. There are, of course, more than ten *defense mechanisms*—a term introduced by Sigmund Freud more than 100 years ago. His daughter Anna Freud continued the journey toward understanding the ego and its defensive nature. Modern thinkers—including Harvard and Dartmouth psychiatrist and researcher George Vaillant, M.D.—in various schools of post-Freudian study took these defense mechanisms and expanded upon them, and they are now recognized by therapists and psychiatrists worldwide.

We thought long and hard about which ones to cover in this book. In the end, we left out some, such as *Distortion* and *Dissociation,* because in their most severe form, they can lead to personality disorders that need professional treatment and are outside the scope of a book such as this.

We also omitted some that you've probably heard and read about and may have a good grasp of: *Acting Out* and *Hypochondria,* for example. Then there's *Suppression,* or "stuffing it." Undoubtedly, it's a common Defender; however, we felt that suppressing uncomfortable wishes, problems, impulses, thoughts, and feelings underlies so many of the other Defenders that we had the idea covered. Understanding how burying our true feelings can isolate us from our loved ones and prevent us from leading a gratifying life, and learning how connecting with our emotions opens us up to acceptance and love, is really the entire message of *Defenders of the Heart.*

We see this book as one that you'll revisit again and again. Pick it up and use our language and some of our ideas when you feel confounded by your own actions. You can reacquaint yourself with your Defender of choice when you find yourself slipping into old patterns. Or perhaps as your life progresses, you'll start to recognize particular behaviors within you and others and will want to find out if what you're coming up against might be a newly identified Defender.

Our wish for you is that this work has illuminated that which has caused you, up until now, to settle for a second-best life. Paying sharper attention to your Defenders of the Heart will lead you to a life that is blue-ribbon in every way.

We'd love to hear from you and find out how you're navigating your way through your Defenders. Share your Talk Story with us. Please visit our Website at: **www. defendersoftheheart.com**.

BIBLIOGRAPHY AND RECOMMENDED RESOURCES

The following are a few of the books that we have tapped into over the course of writing *Defenders of the Heart* (we've included a couple of CDs, too). Some of the works are clinical; others are just downright interesting and speak to anyone who is curious to keep learning, as we are. Several are classics that have stood the test of time, and a few have been reissued or updated over the years. Enjoy them, and know that you'll find something within their pages that you can take to heart.

— Amen, D., and Routh, L. *Healing Anxiety and Depression*. New York: G.P. Putnam's Sons, 2003.

— Bassett, L. *From Panic to Power: Proven Techniques to Calm Your Anxieties, Conquer Your Fears, and Put You in Control of Your Life*. New York: HarperCollins, 1996.

— Benson, H. *The Relaxation Response*. New York: William Morrow and Company, 1975. Updated by Harper Paperbacks, 2000.

— Bliss, E. *Doing it Now.* New York: Bantam, 1984.

— Borysenko, J. Z. *Inner Peace for Busy People.* Carlsbad: Hay House, 2001.

— Borysenko, J. Z., and Campbell, D. *Inner Peace for Busy People: Music To Relax and Renew.* Audio CD. Boulder, CO: Spring Hill, 2001.

— Bowlby, J. *Attachment and Loss, Vol. I: Attachment.* New York: Basic Books, 1969. Reissued 1983.

— Bowlby, J. *Attachment and Loss, Vol. II: Separation: Anxiety and Anger.* New York: Basic Books, 1973.

— Branden, N. *The Art of Living Consciously: The Power of Awareness to Transform Everyday Life.* New York: Fireside, 1997.

— Burns, D. D. *Feeling Good: The New Mood Therapy.* New York: HarperCollins, 1999.

— Casement, P. *Learning From the Patient.* New York: The Guilford Press, 1985. Reissued 1991.

— Cramer, P. *Protecting the Self: Defense Mechanisms in Action.* New York: The Guilford Press, 2006.

— Freud, A. *The Ego and the Mechanisms of Defense.* London: Hogarth, 1936.

— Haan, N. *Coping and Defending.* New York: Academic Press, 1977.

— Hanh, T. N. *The Miracle of Mindfulness.* Boston: Beacon Press, 1999.

— Jeffers, S. *Feel the Fear . . . and Do It Anyway.* New York: Ballantine Books, 1987. Reissued anniversary edition, 2007.

— Kabat-Zinn, J. *Wherever You Go, There You Are: Mindful Meditation in Everyday Life.* New York: Hyperion, 1994.

— Kantor, M. *Passive-Aggression: A Guide for the Therapist, the Patient and the Victim.* New York: Praeger, 2002.

— Kornfield, J. *After the Ecstasy, the Laundry: How the Heart Grows Wise on the Spiritual Path.* New York: Bantam Books, 2000.

— Kornfield, J. *Guided Meditation: Six Essential Practices to Cultivate Love, Awareness, and Wisdom.* Audio CD. Louisville, CO: Sounds True, 2007.

— Kornfield, J. *Meditation for Beginners.* Audio CD. Louisville, CO: Sounds True, 2001.

— Linn, D. *Complete Relaxation.* Audio CD. Carlsbad: Hay House, 2006.

— Mitchell, S. A., and Black, M. J. *Freud and Beyond.* New York: Basic Books, 1995.

— Murphy, T., and Oberlin, L. H. *Overcoming Passive-Aggression: How to Stop Hidden Anger from Spoiling Your Relationship, Career and Happiness.* New York: Marlow & Company, 2005.

— Stern, D. *The Interpersonal World of the Infant.* New York: Basic Books, 1985. Reissued 2000.

— Vaillant, G. *Ego Mechanisms of Defense: A Guide for Clinicians and Researchers.* Washington, D.C.: American Psychiatric Publishing, Inc., 1992.

— Wetzler, S. *Living with the Passive-Aggressive Man.* New York: Fireside, 1992.

ACKNOWLEDGMENTS

So many people have touched our hearts and have been in our corner as this book took its twists and turns. *Defenders of the Heart* took us away from time with friends and family, and we thank you for your patience.

From Marilyn and Neil:

A big thanks to the talented clinicians who added their input, their cheerleading, and their insight: Dr. Terry Eagan; Melissa Capin-Canick, M.F.T.; Dr. Shirley Brazda; Dr. Dani Levine; and the rest of the gang at our Pico office.

We thank our friends, supervisors, confidants, and therapists extraordinaire Dr. Elaine Chaisson and Dr. Michael Mullin.

Peggy Pope, Kenny and Andrea Gootnick, Ben and Julie Simon, Rochel Blachman, Martine and Joao Serro,

Roger and Cheryl Bloxberg, Tim and Robin Davila, Jill Kaufman, Barry Hoffner, Darren Levine, Jim Pathman, and Steve Kishineff: thanks for always being there with a generous heart, support, and belief in us.

Thank you to Byron Laursen for your creative thinking.

Michael Ebeling and Kristina Holmes at Ebeling & Associates: your talent as agents got us on the right path. Thank you.

Thanks to Jill Kramer at Hay House, who believed in this project with full enthusiasm.

To Angela Hynes, our newest and dear friend, with warmth and gratitude for being instrumental in organizing our ramblings and adding invaluable ideas.

We're so appreciative of all those people we interviewed who made it into our hearts but unfortunately not into the pages of our book.

Thanks are due to Pam Ogus for her ten magic fingers.

Our siblings deserve our gratitude—they helped us build our own Defenders: Susie and Steve Schwartz, Larry and Wendy Einbund, Mark and Molly Einbund, Terri and Phil Adam, Anita and Loretta Greenberg, and Bill and Sylvia Greenberg.

To Howard Gordon and Joannie Burstein: thanks for your belief in this project.

To our patients: we have been honored to become a part of your lives and hearts.

From Marilyn:

To Alan Duncan Ross, once partner, now pal: thanks for your quick wit and verbiage, which kicked us into new ideas.

To my darling daughter, Mali, who was—and always will be—tied to me through that special red thread: we are connected for life. With you I have watched Defenders grow and weaken as you take steps out of childhood to adolescence. How lucky we are to have found one another.

To all the listeners who tuned in over the years to *The Marilyn Kagan Show* on KFI: thank you for sharing your deepest, darkest thoughts and concerns night after night.

From Neil:

To my firstborn, Spencer Samuel, who changed my world forever and has taught me how to open my heart further than I ever thought possible. To my stunning and athletic middle daughter, Olivia Michelle, whose spirit, unending determination, and love of competition inspires me to new heights of self-challenge. To my baby, Sophie Rose, who never stops smiling; has an amazingly loving heart and old soul; and has taught me that love can heal all kinds of "boo-boos," even those you can't see but you definitely feel. There's never a day that goes by that I don't thank God for having the pleasure and privilege to share my home, love, laughter, tears, and life with you three.

My love, admiration, and thanks to my father, Merv Einbund, for being my role model and my biggest fan every single day of my life.

My appreciation to the incredible communities of Heschel West Day School and New Community Jewish High School, my extended family, who on a daily basis nurture and educate not only my beautiful children but also our entire family in the ways of respect, tolerance, human decency, and giving back to make the world a better place.

To my wife, Judy, whom I adore, respect, admire, and thank for sharing my life, love, and heart all these years. Without your support, guidance, and wisdom, I would not be half the man I am today. You rock!

We are happy to donate a percentage of *Defenders of the Heart*'s profits to cancer research.

ABOUT THE AUTHORS

Marilyn Kagan, LCSW, has been in private practice for over 25 years. She is well known and respected as one of the media's most sought-after psychological experts. Her popular talk show on Los Angeles radio station KFI aired for seven years, and she hosted the Emmy-nominated *The Marilyn Kagan Show* for three years. Additionally, she's been a frequent commentator on all of the major television networks, including a stint as guest host on E!'s *Talk Soup*.

Neil Einbund, Ph.D., is a licensed clinical psychologist and marriage and family therapist who has been in private practice since 1988. His expertise covers a wide range of specialties, including family dynamics/relationships, marriage counseling, addictions, divorce, and grief work. For the last 20 years, he's taught in the "Making Marriage Work" program at the American Jewish University, where he works in partnership with Marilyn Kagan.

NOTES

NOTES

NOTES

NOTES

NOTES

NOTES

NOTES

NOTES

NOTES

NOTES

NOTES

NOTES

NOTES

NOTES

We hope you enjoyed this Hay House book. If you'd like to receive a free catalog featuring additional Hay House books and products, or if you'd like information about the Hay Foundation, please contact:

Hay House, Inc.
P.O. Box 5100
Carlsbad, CA 92018-5100

(760) 431-7695 or (800) 654-5126
(760) 431-6948 (fax) or (800) 650-5115 (fax)
www.hayhouse.com® • www.hayfoundation.org

Published and distributed in Australia by: Hay House Australia Pty. Ltd., 18/36 Ralph St., Alexandria NSW 2015 • *Phone:* 612-9669-4299 *Fax:* 612-9669-4144 • www.hayhouse.com.au

Published and distributed in the United Kingdom by: Hay House UK, Ltd., 292B Kensal Rd., London W10 5BE • *Phone:* 44-20-8962-1230 • *Fax:* 44-20-8962-1239 • www.hayhouse.co.uk

Published and distributed in the Republic of South Africa by: Hay House SA (Pty), Ltd., P.O. Box 990, Witkoppen 2068 • *Phone/Fax:* 27-11-467-8904 • orders@psdprom.co.za • www.hayhouse.co.za

Published in India by: Hay House Publishers India, Muskaan Complex, Plot No. 3, B-2, Vasant Kunj, New Delhi 110 070 • *Phone:* 91-11-4176-1620 • *Fax:* 91-11-4176-1630 • www.hayhouse.co.in

Distributed in Canada by: Raincoast, 9050 Shaughnessy St., Vancouver, B.C. V6P 6E5 • *Phone:* (604) 323-7100 *Fax:* (604) 323-2600 • www.raincoast.com

Tune in to **HayHouseRadio.com**® for the best in inspirational talk radio featuring top Hay House authors! And, sign up via the Hay House USA Website to receive the Hay House online newsletter and stay informed about what's going on with your favorite authors. You'll receive bimonthly announcements about Discounts and Offers, Special Events, Product Highlights, Free Excerpts, Giveaways, and more!
www.hayhouse.com®